Our Catholic Prayer

Our Catholic Prayer

A Popular Guidebook

Therese Johnson Borchard

A Crossroad Book
The Crossroad Publishing Company
New York

The Crossroad Publishing Company
370 Lexington Avenue, New York, NY 10017

Acknowledgments are found on pp. 142-144, which constitute an extension of the copyright page.

Printed in the United States of America

Library of Congress Cataloging-in-Publication Data

Borchard, Therese Johnson.
Our Catholic prayer : a popular guidebook / Therese Johnson Borchard.
p. cm.
Includes bibliographical references.
ISBN 0-8245-1606-0 (pbk.)
1. Prayer—Catholic Church. I. Title.
BV210.2.B647 1999 98-46462
248.3—dc21 CIP

1 2 3 4 5 6 7 8 9 10 04 03 02 01 00 99

For Father David E. Schlaver, C.S.C.,
friend and spiritual director,
who has taught me about prayer
by his wonderful example.

Contents

INTRODUCTION: *What Is Prayer?* 9

ONE: *The Lord's Prayer* 17

TWO: *Forms of Prayer* 33

THREE: *Communal Prayer* 53

FOUR: *Private Prayer* 69

FIVE: *Meditation and Contemplation* 81

SIX: *Lectio Divina* 101

SEVEN: *The Language of Prayer* 115

EIGHT: *The Body and Prayer* 127

WORKS CITED 139

ACKNOWLEDGMENTS 142

INTRODUCTION

What Is Prayer?

For me, prayer is a surge of the heart; it is a simple look turned toward heaven, it is a cry of recognition and of love, embracing both trial and joy.

—Thérèse of Lisieux

I cannot begin a book on prayer without first quoting my patron saint, Thérèse of Lisieux. Her definition of prayer—better yet, her entire life—describes prayer in its fullest meaning: a look toward heaven, a cry of love, and a joyful embrace.

Other classic definitions of prayer include that of St. John Damascene, who said prayer is "raising the mind to God," and St. Gregory of Nyssa, who considered prayer as "conversation and discussion with God."

Of course there are more contemporary definitions of prayer, such as the one John Macquarrie gives—"Prayer is thinking,"—and that of Lawrence Cunningham: "Prayer is . . . that basic relation between God and the person who encounters God." The late Swiss theologian Hans Urs von Balthasar described prayer as "an exchange between God and the soul."

The *New Catholic Encyclopedia* offers three definitions of prayer that are found in every age of Christianity:

> Prayer . . . is, in the strict sense, the filial expression of one's desires for self and others to the heavenly Father from whom come all good things, natural or supernatural. In a wider sense it is the ascent of the mind to God; and in the widest sense it is speaking with God.

As a basic definition, however, and one that resonates best with my own experience of prayer, I go to *The HarperCollins Encyclopedia of Catholicism* (referred to hereafter as the *Encyclopedia of Catholicism*) that defines prayer as "the act by which one enters into conscious, loving communion with God."

KINDS OF PRAYER

The English word *prayer* comes from the Latin verb *precari*, which means "to entreat or beg." In this literal sense, prayer means a petition or request. However, petition is just one kind of prayer in the word's wider sense. Prayer is also adoration, praise, thanksgiving, intercession, and repentance.

Adoration, praise, and thanksgiving are all similar in that they respond to the blessings and abundance our Creator has generously bestowed on us. Prayers of adoration and praise acknowledge the greatness of God as the maker of all creation; prayers of thanksgiving are said in gratitude for individual and collective gifts.

Prayers of petition, intercession, and repentance are related in that they remind us of our weakness and inadequacies. They are said in humility, as a response to our neediness before God.

METHODS OF PRAYER

Not only are there different kinds of prayer to consider, there are various expressions or methods of prayer.

For example, vocal prayer uses words and gestures as media of expression, while mental prayer is a movement within—involving mind, imagination, and will in a reflective process.

There is private prayer, in which an individual addresses God alone, and communal prayer—including liturgical prayer—in which a group of people pray together.

Two final methods worth mentioning here are meditation and contemplation. Although the two terms are often used interchangeably, there is a slight distinction between the two: meditative prayer involves discursive reasoning, while contemplative prayer takes us beyond what the rational faculties can access.

THE VALUE OF PRAYER

Having explored a few definitions of prayer and reviewing some kinds and methods, it is time to consider this very important question: Why pray? There must be some inherent value in prayer or else people would not devote so much time toward it. What are these benefits? The *Encyclopedia of Catholicism* explains:

> By praying, individuals are changed, raised to a new level of spiritual being that affects understanding and behavior. Increase in virtue should be the fruit of praying. Interaction with other people should be marked by greater

> charity, compassion, and willingness to be of service. A new freedom from deep-rooted, self-centered attachments begins to emerge. Selfishness gives way to an awareness of others that is based on deeper awareness of God. Perceptions are cleansed and capacities for joy are increased.

Similarly, the *New Catholic Encyclopedia* states:

> Praying furnishes the intellect with religious knowledge; produces in the will sentiments of admiration, respect, fear, joy, and desire for God; and makes the virtues of faith, hope, and charity more vital and dynamic in a person's life.

Finally, John H. Wright, S.J., writes:

> Prayer is like the symbolic activity of words and gestures by which human beings bring to expression their personal relationships to one another.
>
> But these words and gestures among human beings do not merely express and embody existing relationships; they also initiate, sustain, modify, and intensify them. As symbolic activity, they are effective, they produce a result. . . . So, too, prayer accepts, deepens, and intensifies my relationship with God, the relationship he intends and initiates. ("Prayer" in *The New Dictionary of Catholic Spirituality*)

QUALITIES OF TRUE PRAYER

Prayer has to be of a certain quality, however, to earn the benefits just described. In order for our prayer to be effective, we must follow the guidelines laid out by Jesus when he taught his disciples how to pray.

The most important requirement is to pray with faith. Jesus tells his disciples in the Gospel of Mark:

> Have faith in God. Truly I tell you, if you say to this mountain, "Be taken up and thrown into the sea," and if you do not doubt in your heart, but believe that what you say will come to pass, it will be done for you. So, I tell you, whatever you ask for in prayer, believe that you have received it, and it will be yours. (Mark 11:22-24)

We must also pray attentively.

> I will pray with the spirit, but I will pray with the mind also; I will sing praise with the spirit, but I will sing praise with the mind also. (1 Cor. 14:15)

And always, we must pray with perseverance.

> Jesus told [his disciples] a parable about their need to pray always and not to lose heart. (Luke 18:1)

This passage goes on to tell the parable of the judge who granted justice to the widow as a result of her persistent pleas (Luke 18:2-8).

CATHOLIC TRADITION AND PRAYER

In addition to Scripture, we must look to our Church tradition—the transmission of holy wisdom and teachings from one age to the next—in order to learn best how to pray. The *Catechism of the Catholic Church* describes the place of Catholic tradition with regard to prayer:

> Prayer cannot be reduced to the spontaneous outpouring of interior impulse: in order to pray, one must have the will to pray. Nor is it enough to know what the Scriptures reveal about prayer: one must also learn how to pray. Through a living transmission (Sacred Tradition) within the "believing and praying Church" (*Dei Verbum* 8), the Holy Spirit teaches the children of God how to pray.
>
> The tradition of Christian prayer is one of the ways in which the tradition of faith takes shape and grows, especially through the contemplation and study of believers who treasure in their hearts the events and words of the economy of salvation, and through their profound grasp of the spiritual realities they experience (*Dei Verbum* 8).

Guided by the words of Scripture, Catholic tradition, the Church fathers, and today's theologians, I present in this book an overview or summary of Catholic prayer. Each of the eight chapters includes a brief history and theology on its topic as well as classic and contemporary meditations.

My hope is that this book provides you with a better understanding of Catholic prayer, while encouraging you to learn more about prayer on your own.

CHAPTER ONE

The Lord's Prayer

The Lord's Prayer is the most perfect of prayers. . . . In it we ask, not only for all the things we can rightly desire, but also in the sequence that they should be desired. This prayer not only teaches us to ask for things, but also in what order we should desire them.

—Thomas Aquinas

HISTORY OF THE LORD'S PRAYER

The Lord's Prayer is without doubt the best known and most loved of all Christian prayers. It is the model of all Christian prayer, as it was first recited by Jesus to his disciples as an example of how they are to pray. This prayer forever holds a special place in the hearts of all believers.

The Lord's Prayer is also known as the "Our Father," or in Latin the *Pater Noster*, named from the opening words of the prayer.

TWO VERSIONS

Two versions of the Lord's Prayer exist in the New Testament. The first appears in the Gospel of Matthew (6:9b-13), and is situated in the middle of the Sermon on the Mount. It is introduced by Jesus' words, "Pray then in this way" (Matt. 6:9a). The second appears in the Gospel of Luke (11:2b-4), and is a response to one of the disciples' request: "Lord, teach us to pray, as John taught his disciples" (Luke 11:1b). Matthew's prayer consists of the address ("Our Father in heaven") and seven petitions. Luke's prayer is shorter, including an address ("Father") and five petitions.

Most modern forms of the prayer are based on

THE LORD'S PRAYER

NEW REVISED STANDARD VERSION OF THE BIBLE

• *Matthew 6:9b-13*

Our Father in heaven,
hallowed be your name.
Your kingdom come.
Your will be done,
    on earth as it is in heaven.
Give us this day our daily bread.
And forgive us our debts,
    as we also have forgiven our debtors.
And do not bring us to the time of trial,
    but rescue us from the evil one.

• *Luke 11:2b-4*

Father, hallowed be your name.
Your kingdom come.
Give us each day our daily bread.
And forgive us our sins,
    for we ourselves forgive everyone
    indebted to us.
And do not bring us to the time of trial.

Matthew's version; however, that is not to say that Matthew's prayer is more authentic. Both versions are important because—as Nicholas Ayo writes in *The Lord's Prayer*—"they give us two portraits of the same prayer, just as the gospels offer four portraits of the same Jesus."

THE DOXOLOGY

Some manuscripts of Matthew add a doxology to the prayer. Variations of the words "For thine is the kingdom and the power and the glory. Amen" are a common conclusion to the prayer, especially in Reformed traditions. The Roman Mass now includes this doxology as a separate communal prayer after the recitation of the Lord's Prayer.

EARLY CHURCH COMMUNITY

It is clear from Paul's letters and from what is written in the *Didache*—a book of Christian instruction dating back to the first century—that the Lord's Prayer had already become the liturgical prayer of the early Christian community by the first century. Paul's letters, the *Didache*, and the Gospels point to the prominent place of this prayer in early Christian worship. It began to replace other prayers—such as the "Eighteen Benedictions"—customary in Jewish piety.

THEOLOGY OF THE LORD'S PRAYER

Saint Thomas Aquinas referred to the Lord's Prayer in his *Summa Theologica* as the "perfect prayer." Tertullian, in a third-century commentary, described it as "the summary of the whole gospel." And Saint Augustine, after some discussion on the psalms, writes:

> Run through all the words of the holy prayers [in Scripture], and I do not think that you will find anything in them that is not contained and included in the Lord's Prayer. (St. Augustine, *Ep.* 130, 12, 22: *Patrologia Latina* 33, 503, as quoted in the *Catechism of the Catholic Church*, no. 2762)

A SUMMARY OF THE GOSPEL

The Lord's Prayer, is, indeed, a summary of the Gospels. It is the nuts and bolts of Jesus' message, the heart and soul of his teaching, in that it first praises God, whom Jesus calls Father, and then presents petitions of need in a spirit of humility.

The petitions are basic: for nourishment and sustenance, for forgiveness and reconciliation among people, and for deliverance from evil. And the coming of the kingdom of God is a particularly important theme in the prayer.

The theology of the Lord's Prayer is well summarized in the *Encyclopedia of Catholicism*:

> The heart of the prayer is a petition that God make the kingdom, or divine sovereign authority over humankind, a present reality. In the interim, the petitioner asks for physical sustenance, reconciliation with God and neighbor, and preservation from temptation and evil.

THE COMING OF THE KINGDOM

In order to best understand and pray the Lord's Prayer, it is important to know what is meant by *eschatology*. Nicholas Ayo offers an appropriate definition of eschatology in light of the Lord's Prayer:

> The *eschaton* in Greek refers to the last things or the last days. An eschatological approach suggests the final times, the resurrection of the dead, the fulfillment which God has already begun on earth in Jesus Christ who is Lord and who will judge the world. . . . Christians await the *second* coming of Christ, and they pray the Our Father in the light of the first coming of the Lord. (*The Lord's Prayer*)

Ayo goes on to quote the late biblical scholar Raymond Brown, who explains how the early

Christian community read and prayed the Lord's Prayer with regard to the coming of Christ:

> The Christian community of the first century, anxiously expecting the Second Coming, prays that God will completely glorify His name by establishing His kingdom, which represents the fulfillment of the plan He has willed for both earth and heaven. For its portion in this consummation of time, the community asks a place at the heavenly banquet table to break bread with Christ, and a forgiveness of its sins. A titanic struggle with Satan stands between the community and the realization of its prayer, and from this it asks to be delivered. ("The Pater Noster as an Eschatological Prayer," *Theological Studies*, as quoted in *The Lord's Prayer*)

GOD AS FATHER

Also theologically significant in the Lord's Prayer is Jesus' addressing God as "Father." Jesus was the first to use the intimate address *Abba*, an Aramaic term used by the Jewish community in everyday life within the family. This way of speaking to God was unique to Jesus, and was characteristic of his theology: Jesus was now the new way of relating to God, but the disciples were invited to share in this loving bond by addressing God together with Jesus as "Father." United with

Christ, believers enter into a special relationship with God as children.

This familiar form of addressing God—and the special relationship it symbolized—were adopted early on into the liturgical life of the first Church communities.

THE SEVEN PETITIONS

There are seven petitions included in Matthew's prayer, the version that has been accepted into the liturgical tradition of the Church. The *Catechism of the Catholic Church* groups the petitions into two series and offers a summary of them:

> The first series of petitions carries us toward him, for his own sake: *thy* name, *thy* kingdom, *thy* will! . . . These three supplications were already answered in the saving sacrifice of Christ, but they are henceforth directed in hope toward their final fulfillment.
>
> The second series of petitions unfolds with the same movement as certain Eucharistic epicleses: as an offering up of our expectations, that draws down upon itself the eyes of the Father of mercies. They go up from us and concern us from this very moment, in our present world: "give *us* . . . forgive *us* . . . lead *us* not . . . deliver *us*. . . ." (*Catechism of the Catholic Church*, no. 2805-06)

THE SEVEN PETITIONS

- *The First Petition:*
  Hallowed be Thy name

- *The Second Petition:*
  Thy kingdom come

- *The Third Petition:*
  Thy will be done on earth as it is in Heaven

- *The Fourth Petition:*
  Give us this day our daily bread

- *The Fifth Petition:*
  And forgive us our debts, as we also forgive our debtors

- *The Sixth Petition:*
  And lead us not into temptation

- *The Seventh Petition:*
  But deliver us from evil

There are numerous commentaries and meditations on the Seven Petitions. One of the classics is that of the late German theologian Romano Guardini. The following passages are excerpted from his *The Lord's Prayer*.

Hallowed be Thy name

In this, His name, God moves through the language of man, through his heart and mouth and destiny; and the holy name shares the fate of all words.

Thy kingdom come

The second petition of the Lord's Prayer leads us into the very core of what lay nearest to the heart of Jesus. In the form in which it is most used, the words are "Thy kingdom come!" But this is not an absolutely exact translation of the words. Actually it should be "May Thy kingdom arrive" or "May Thy kingdom come." If we say them this way, we feel their vital sense distinctly. There is expectation in them, as well as yearning. Something salutary is far away, and the petition implores that it may come. There is a movement in process, and the longing urges that it may be accomplished.

Thy will be done on earth as it is in Heaven

The prayer asks that His will be done here on earth, where we do not see His light, just as if we did see it—namely, by faith. It asks that although we have not seen, we may love.

Give us this day our daily bread

[This petition] refers us to what underlies the Christian day and the Christian trust: the mystery of Divine Providence.

And forgive us our debts, as we also forgive our debtors

Being a Christian means . . . continually rising up out of guilt—the one great common guilt, together with all it includes of our individual guilt—to come to God and beg him for forgiveness; and it means being gradually transformed by this continually renewed forgiveness.

And lead us not into temptation

This petition of the Lord's Prayer knows that [temptation] can happen and that God is only being just when He permits it. But it calls upon that quality in God that is greater than His justice—namely, His mercy.

But deliver us from evil

At the end of Revelation, the cry, "Come, Lord Jesus!" arises out of the company of those awaiting the Lord. Out of the depths of the petition, "Deliver us from evil," the selfsame cry resounds. . . . It is the inmost core of the created world, which sighs for God, and "groans and travails in pain" for the coming of the last things.

THE LORD'S PRAYER TODAY

The Lord's Prayer continues to hold a special place today both in the private devotional lives of the faithful and in the sacramental life of the Church.

THE PRAYER OF THE CHURCH

From very early times unto our day, the Lord's Prayer has played a special role in the sacraments of initiation: Baptism, Confirmation, and Eucharist. It was the first Christian prayer given to the catechumen preparing to be received into the Church. According to St. John Chrysostom and the apostolic tradition, the Lord's Prayer is essentially a liturgical prayer, to be prayed in the context of the universal Church:

> [The Lord] teaches us to make prayer in common for all our brethren. For he did not say "my Father" who art in heaven, but "our" Father, offering petitions for the common Body. (St. John Chrysostom, *Hom. in Mt.* 19, 4: *Patrologia Graeca* 57, 278, as quoted in the *Catechism of the Catholic Church*, no. 2768)

The *Catechism of the Catholic Church* calls the Lord's Prayer "the prayer of the Church."

> The Lord's Prayer is the quintessential prayer of the Church. It is an integral part of the major hours of the Divine Office and of the sacraments of Christian initiation: Baptism, Confirmation, and Eucharist. Integrated into the Eucharist it reveals the eschatological character of its petitions, hoping for the Lord, "until he comes" (1 Cor. 11:26).

THE PRAYER OF INTEGRAL LIBERATION

As the great mystics and spiritual writers of the past found new meanings in the words of the Lord's Prayer, so too do religious thinkers of our era seek original ways of interpreting and praying this ancient prayer.

A wonderful example of a unique reading of the prayer is the one presented by Leonardo Boff in his *The Lord's Prayer: The Prayer of Integral Liberation.* A key figure in Latin American liberation theology, Boff offers the Lord's Prayer as a model of right relationship between the Creator and creation.

> In the Lord's Prayer we encounter in a practical way the correct relationship between God and humankind, between heaven and earth, between the religious and the political, while maintaining unity throughout. The first part speaks on God's behalf: the Father, keeping his name holy, his kingdom, his holy will. The

> second part is concerned with human interests: our daily bread, forgiveness, ever-present temptation, and ever-threatening evil.
>
> The two parts constitute the one prayer of Jesus. God is not just interested in what belongs to him: his name, his kingdom, his divine will. He is also concerned about our affairs: bread, forgiveness, temptation, evil. Likewise we are not just concerned with what is vital to us. . . . We are also open to the Father's concerns: sanctification of God's name, the coming of God's kingdom, the realization of God's will.

SUMMARY OF THE LORD'S PRAYER

After pointing out some alternative readings of the Lord's Prayer, Nicholas Ayo summarizes the readings into two categories: the eschatological and the everyday. The eschatological emphasizes the eternal or transcendent nature of the prayer, while the everyday concentrates on the temporal, imminent meaning. According to Ayo, "Matthew's text lends itself to an end-time and spiritual reading of the Lord's Prayer, and Luke's to a more literal and daily life orientation."

Ayo goes on to present a summary of his own commentary on the Lord's Prayer. His eight statements form an excellent overview of the prayer, and an appropriate conclusion to our chapter.

NICHOLAS AYO
THE LORD'S PRAYER

• *The Lord's Prayer is a* ***collect*** *prayer.*

The total impact of the Our Father is not only the sum of the three thou-petitions and the three we-petitions. The whole is more than the sum of its parts. The Pater is a prayer that sums up or "collects" all other prayers.

• *The Lord's Prayer is a* ***recognition*** *prayer.*

Its petitions state the way things are. The words of the Pater present the simple truth. This is who God is; this is what we must have.

• *The Lord's Prayer is a* ***mystical*** *prayer.*

The text of the Pater is a school for the spiritual life. The eastern fathers and the western teachers of spirituality saw in these few words a concise guide to the development of the Christian life of holiness and union with God.

• *The Lord's Prayer is a prayer of* ***perpetual mercy***.

Believers in the Father's love can afford unlimited mercy because they are rich in God's mercy.

• *The Lord's Prayer is an* ***eschatological*** *prayer, a resurrection prayer.*

This is the day the Lord has made. This is a new day of creation, like the first day that knew no past.

• *The Lord's Prayer is a* ***doxological*** *prayer.*

Petition becomes doxology as the Many is enfolded in the One.

• *The Lord's Prayer is a* ***repetitious*** *prayer.*

It is so not only because we repeat its words so many times in a lifetime, but also because it says only one thing. Let the Father be Abba; may God be God.

• *The Lord's Prayer is a* ***simple*** *prayer.*

There is only one prayer and only one petition. May God be God. "Abba, Father."

CHAPTER TWO

FORMS OF PRAYER

All forms of prayer belong together. . . . Adoration and repentance, yearning and praise, thanksgiving and communion, petition and reverence, are all interconnected. They are but different aspects of the living relationship of man to God.

—Romano Guardini

HISTORY OF THE FORMS OF PRAYER

The Lord's Prayer is perhaps called the perfect prayer because it introduces the believer to all of the primary forms of prayer: adoration, praise, thanksgiving, petition, intercession, and repentance. In the simple prayer that Jesus taught us rests the foundation for all the basic kinds of prayer. We praise, honor, and thank our Creator; we beg forgiveness; and we place our needs before God, asking to be heard.

ADORATION

According to Romano Guardini, adoration is the "proper response to God's goodness." It is "one of the highest attitudes of prayer" (*Encyclopedia of Catholicism*). The *New Catholic Encyclopedia* defines adoration as:

> The reverential attitude of man toward God, by which he acknowledges, with his whole being, soul and body, God's absolute immensity, holiness, and glory and subjects himself to Him with such intensity that this disposition manifests itself in proper words and perceptible physical acts. Adoration . . . is the directing of one's whole being toward God, so that in all its diversity it is to the praise and glory of God.

The Old and New Testaments are full of prayers of adoration. A beautiful passage describing the intensity of pure adoration is found in the fourth chapter of the Book of Revelations:

> Holy, holy, holy,
> the Lord God the Almighty,
> who was and is and is to come. (Rev. 4:8b)
>
> You are worthy, our Lord and God,
> to receive glory and honor and power,
> for you created all things. (Rev. 4:11)

PRAISE

Like prayers of adoration, prayers of praise draw the believer's attention to the greatness of God. Praise happens when the pray-er rejoices in God and glorifies God. We need only to look to the Book of Psalms to find examples of this kind of prayer in Scripture. Throughout the Psalms, glory is given to God on behalf of God's work in creation—the beauty of nature—and God's wondrous deeds in history.

Following is Psalm 148, the last of the Psalms of creation (which includes Psalms 18, 103, 104, and 148). The author of this psalm calls upon all created things to praise the Lord:

Praise the Lord!
Praise the Lord from the heavens;
    praise him in the heights!
Praise him, all his angels;
    praise him, all his host!
Praise him, sun and moon;
    praise him, all you shining stars!
Praise him, you highest heavens,
    and you waters above the heavens!
Let them praise the name of the Lord,
    for he commanded and they were created.
(Ps. 148:1-5)

THANKSGIVING

John Wright groups prayers of praise and thanksgiving together in his book *A Theology of Christian Prayer* when he says:

> The most characteristic and fundamental response to the presence and action of God in the world, as given in sacred Scripture, is the prayer of praise and thanksgiving.

The only distinction he makes between the two kinds of prayer is this:

> Psalms of praise . . . acknowledge the power of God at work in establishing and maintaining the universal context in which human life is lived, the context of both nature and history.

> Psalms of gratitude concentrate on particular favors bestowed on an individual, or occasionally on the community.

Romano Guardini explains that "as soon as prayer is answered it becomes thanksgiving. . . . it is man's response to God's grace." When we say prayers of thanksgiving and gratitude, we change our orientation: we go outside of ourselves to acknowledge another.

> Gratitude and thanksgiving are both radically self-transcendent attitudes and acts by which we orient ourselves toward another in recognition of the other's freely given gift, favor, or care. (*The New Dictionary of Christian Spirituality*)

The Psalms, again, and much of the Old and New Testaments abound in hymns of thanksgiving and gratitude. In his letters to various communities, the apostle Paul reminds believers to give thanks to God and to always be grateful. He says to the Colossians:

> Be thankful . . . and with gratitude in your hearts sing psalms, hymns, and spiritual songs to God. And whatever you do . . . do everything in the name of the Lord Jesus, giving thanks to God the Father through him. (Col. 3:15-17)

PETITION

As mentioned briefly in the introduction, the word *prayer* means literally a petition or request. Although prayer is also adoration, praise, thanksgiving, intercession, and repentance, in its strictest sense it is petition.

The *New Dictionary of Catholic Spirituality* defines petition as:

> a fundamental stance before the mystery of God. It arises at the intersection of human need . . . and the religious belief in a caring "Other" who desires what is for human good.

Psalm 86 serves as a wonderful example of this form of prayer:

> Incline your ear, O Lord, and answer me,
> for I am poor and needy.
> Preserve my life, for I am devoted to you;
> save your servant who trusts in you.
> You are my God; be gracious to me, O Lord,
> for to you do I cry all day long.
> Gladden the soul of your servant,
> for to you, O Lord, I lift up my soul.
> For you, O Lord, are good and forgiving,
> abounding in steadfast love to all who call
> on you.
> Give ear, O Lord, to my prayer;
> listen to my cry of supplication.

> In the day of my trouble I call on you,
> for you will answer me. (Ps. 86:1-7)

INTERCESSION

Prayers of intercession are like prayers of petition in that a person "seeks the help of God for a special favor" (*Encyclopedia of Catholicism*). However, intercessory prayer is unique to all other kinds of prayer in that "the benefit sought is for another" (*New Catholic Encyclopedia*). According to P. J. Mahoney, intercession is:

> the act of pleading by one who in God's sight has a right to do so in order to obtain mercy for one in need. (*New Catholic Encyclopedia*)

He further explains that the intercessor acts as a defense attorney, an advocate, pleading on behalf of another; the intercessor, then, must be in good standing with God.

Examples of intercessory prayer run through the entire Hebrew Scriptures. In the stories of the Old Testament, God is raising up leaders to speak on behalf of the people. These prophets, kings, and priests "call the people back to God and intercede for them in their sins" (*The New Dictionary of Catholic Spirituality*).

Andrew D. Ciferni, O. Praem., cites the

Suffering Servant passage of Isaiah as "the paradigm of intercessory prayer in the Hebrew Scriptures" (*The New Dictionary of Catholic Spirituality*).

> Surely he has borne our infirmities
> and carried our diseases;
> yet we accounted him stricken,
> struck down by God, and afflicted.
> But he was wounded for our transgressions,
> crushed for our iniquities;
> upon him was the punishment that made us whole,
> and by his bruises we are healed. . . .
> Therefore I will allot him a portion with the great,
> and he shall divide the spoil with the strong;
> because he poured out himself to death,
> and was numbered with the transgressors;
> yet he bore the sin of many,
> and made intercession for the transgressors.
> (Isa. 53:4-5, 12)

REPENTANCE

In his book *The Art of Praying*, Romano Guardini writes that "the first motive for prayer springs from man's awareness of his own unworthiness before the holiness of God." He goes on to describe the prayer of repentance:

> Man recognizes that he is selfish, unjust, deficient, and impure. He acknowledges his own wrongdoings and tries to assess them: not merely those of today or of yesterday, but of the whole of his life. Beyond this he tries to visualize the whole of the human condition with its shortcomings.

Prayers of repentance, or contrition, are based on the belief that Jesus Christ has provided redemption for human sinfulness. Our prayers do not go unheard; God acknowledges us. When we confess our sins, we remember our dependence on Jesus.

Once again, we return to the Book of Psalms for an example of this kind of prayer:

> Have mercy on me, O God,
> according to your steadfast love;
> according to your abundant mercy
> blot out my transgressions.
> Wash me thoroughly from my iniquity,
> and cleanse me from my sin.
> For I know my transgressions,
> and my sin is ever before me.
> Against you, you alone, have I sinned,
> and done what is evil in your sight,
> so that you are justified in your sentence
> and blameless when you pass judgement.
> (Ps. 51:1-4)

PRAYERS FROM THE TRADITION

• *Prayer of Adoration*

You are holy, Lord, the only God,
and your deeds are wonderful.
You are strong.
You are great.
You are the Most High,
You are almighty.
You, holy Father, are
King of heaven and earth.
You are Three and One,
Lord God, all good.
You are Good, all Good, supreme Good,
Lord God, living and true. . . .

—St. Francis of Assisi

• *Prayer of Praise*

We praise thee, O God: we acknowledge thee to be the Lord.
All the earth doth worship thee: the Father everlasting.
To thee all Angels cry aloud: the Heavens, and all the Powers therein.
To thee Cherubim and Seraphim: continually do cry,
Holy, Holy, Holy: Lord God of Sabaoth;
Heaven and earth are full of the Majesty: of thy Glory.

The glorious company of the Apostles: praise thee.
The goodly fellowship of the Prophets: praise thee.
The noble army of Martyrs: praise thee.
The holy Church throughout all the world: doth acknowledge thee;
The Father: of an infinite Majesty;
Thine honourable, true: and only Son;
Also the Holy Ghost: the Comforter. . . .

—Te Deum Laudamus

• *Prayer of Thanksgiving*

My God and my All! What greater blessing can I receive than your love? What greater wealth can I possess than your grace? What greater pleasure can I enjoy than your presence? What greater sweetness can I taste than your body and blood? What greater wisdom can I know than your gospel?

Your wisdom is so simple that even fools like myself can understand it. Your holy communion is so generously given that even sinners like me are allowed to receive it. Your presence is everywhere so that even someone with such a dull mind as I have can find you. Your grace is such a constant source of reassurance that I can trust you completely for all my spiritual and material needs. And your love is so warm and so forgiving that even a cold, hard heart like my own is melted.

—Thomas à Kempis

• *Prayer of Petition*

God, of your goodness give me yourself for you are sufficient for me. I cannot properly ask anything less, to be worthy of you. If I were to ask less, I should always be in want. In you alone do I have all.

—Julian of Norwich

• *Prayer of Intercession*

We have confidence in you.
You were the creator of all that we see.
And you have opened our inward eyes
To give us knowledge of you,
Who alone are the Most High, in the highest heaven.
The Holy One, holiest amongst the holy.

You curb the schemes of the cunning,
Frustrate the designs of the wicked,
Raise up the meek and humble,
And bring down the mighty and arrogant.
You give riches and poverty, life and death,
According to your own mysterious plan.
You are the Lord of all flesh;
You watch over all that we do;
You protect us from danger;
You lift us from despair.
And through Jesus Christ, your dear child,
You give us truth, holiness and honour. . . .

Give concord and peace to us all.
Grant us health in body and in soul.
Make our rulers wise and righteous,
That their laws may conform to your laws.
You alone have the means to do this
And much more than this, beyond our asking.
Glory and majesty be yours,
Now at this moment,
In every generation,
Age after age.

—Clement of Rome

• *Prayer of Repentance*

Through your whole life, O Lord Jesus Christ, you suffered that I might be saved. And yet your suffering is not at an end. For still you have to bear with me, stumbling as I walk along the path, and constantly going astray. How often have I become impatient, wanting to give up your way! And how often have you given me the encouragement and helping hand that I need. Every day I increase the burden that you must bear; but just as I am impatient so you are infinitely patient.

—Søren Kierkegaard

THEOLOGY OF THE FORMS OF PRAYER

"All forms of prayer belong together," said Romano Guardini, yet each has a unique theology. Petition and intercession, for example, raise theological questions that thanksgiving and praise do not. Volumes could be written on the theologies of the different kinds of prayer. I do not have space in these pages to discuss them in any depth; I offer here, then, a few theological themes that are woven throughout all forms of prayer.

HOLINESS OF GOD

All forms of prayer affirm the holiness of God and assert our monotheistic faith. We praise, thank, adore, and honor our one God because that God is worthy and deserving of glory. In raising up our holy Creator, we acknowledge that we are less than God, that we are human; we make the fair distinction between God, who is perfect, and humans, who are imperfect and in need of God's forgiveness and grace.

Romano Guardini writes, "Adoration affirms: 'Thou art God; I am man. Thou art the One that truly is, self-created, substantial from all eternity. I am only through Thee. . . .'" All kinds of prayer, not only adoration, affirm this statement.

DISCLOSURE OF GOD

John Wright explains in *A Theology of Christian Prayer* that "the basic motives for praise and thanksgiving turn out to be the traditional areas of divine disclosure, the sources of our knowledge of God." These motives and places of divine disclosure are:

> 1) God's action in creation, the world around us;
> 2) the great deeds of God in history;
> 3) personal experience, both in prayer and the rest of one's life as illuminated by prayer;
> 4) communal experience, events, or gatherings in which the people share together.

Not only in praise and thanksgiving, but in all forms of prayer, God discloses the divine nature: namely, perfect love, pure goodness, and endless grace.

SANCTIFICATION

One last theological theme is that of sanctification. In prayer, the believer is transformed and changed to become more like the Ultimate Good that is being disclosed. As a person prays, divine love touches the soul and makes it yearn even more for God.

ROMANO GUARDINI
THE ART OF PRAYING

God is inexhaustible, and man is—to paraphrase an expression used by Anselm of Canterbury—the inexhaustible in the sight of God.

. . . Thus there is prayer which responds to the remoteness of God—to His hiddenness and to His unknownness. Conversely, there is prayer which responds to His nearness, His openness, and His accessibility. There is prayer which springs from the direct comprehension of the truth—prayer which is, as it were, a spontaneous confession of faith.

But there is also prayer which is a confession of ignorance, an admission of failure before the mystery. There is the prayer of plenitude, when God's presence is fully experienced; but there is also the prayer of privation when it appears that God has forsaken us, leaving a great void which nothing can fill.

There are times when everything seems intelligible and familiar, and there are times when nothing seems to make sense or to be worthwhile, when there is no hope and no one to turn to—times when we must persevere in silence. All these different times demand their own forms of prayer.

Yet all forms of prayer belong together. If we were merely conscious of our own unworthiness without the reassuring thought that, in spite of it, we belong to God, we could not pray. On the other hand, when we yearn for God we become acutely aware of our failings and imperfections. If we were to make light of them, our yearning would lack humility. Again, if we were unable to apprehend the glory of God and to rejoice over it, the feeling of His power would overawe us. Then again, when praising God we might easily be led into unseemly flattery unless restrained by the awe which His holiness inspires in us.

Petition and thanksgiving are complementary; they are our way of acknowledging the great mystery of divine love to which we owe our existence. Thus a short reflection teaches us that adoration and repentance, yearning and praise, thanksgiving and communion, petition and reverence, are all interconnected. They are but different aspects of the living relationship of man to God, made possible because God reveals Himself to man and calls him.

FORMS OF PRAYER TODAY

Although the same forms of prayer have been with us since the days of ancient Israel and the first community of Christians, new expressions are continually born that give all kinds of prayers meaning for our age. The *Catechism of the Catholic Church* explains that the source of inspiration for new expression comes from the Holy Spirit:

> The Holy Spirit who teaches the Church and recalls to her all that Jesus said also instructs her in the life of prayer, inspiring new expressions of the same basic forms of prayer: blessing, petition, intercession, thanksgiving, and praise. (*Catechism of the Catholic Church*, no. 2644)

FIVE FORMS OF PRAYER TODAY

I offer here a few excerpts from the *Catechism* because what is written in its pages reflects the spirit of the basic forms of prayer today. The *Catechism* divides prayer into five kinds; the only form of prayer that we have discussed that is not included here is repentance.

CATECHISM OF THE CATHOLIC CHURCH

• *Adoration*

Adoration is the first attitude of man acknowledging that he is a creature before his Creator. It exalts the greatness of the Lord who made us (Ps. 95: 1-6) and the almighty power of the Savior who sets us free from evil. . . . Adoration of the thrice-holy and sovereign God of love blends with humility and gives assurance to our supplications.

• *Petition*

By prayer of petition we express awareness of our relationship with God. We are creatures who are not our own beginning, not the masters of adversity, not our own last end. We are sinners who as Christians know that we have turned away from our Father. Our petition is already a turning back to him.

• *Intercession*

Intercession is a prayer of petition which leads us to pray as Jesus did. He is the one intercessor with the Father on behalf of all men, especially sinners (Rom. 8:34; 1 John 2:1; 1 Tim. 2:5-8). He is "able for all time to save those who draw near to God through him, since he always lives to make intercession for them" (Heb. 7:25). The

Holy Spirit "himself intercedes for us . . . and intercedes for the saints according to the will of God" (Rom. 8:26-27).

• *Thanksgiving*

Thanksgiving characterizes the prayer of the Church which, in celebrating the Eucharist, reveals and becomes more fully what she is. Indeed, in the work of salvation, Christ sets creation free from sin and death to consecrate it anew and make it return to the Father, for his glory. The thanksgiving of the members of the Body participates in that of their Head.

• *Praise*

Praise is the form of prayer which recognizes most immediately that God is God. It lauds God for his own sake and gives him glory, quite beyond what he does, but simply because *he is*. It shares in the blessed happiness of the pure of heart who love God in faith before seeing him in glory. By praise, the Spirit is joined to our spirits to bear witness that we are children of God (Rom. 8:16), testifying to the only Son in whom we are adopted and by whom we glorify the Father. Praise embraces the other forms of prayer and carries them toward him who is its source and goal.

CHAPTER THREE

Communal Prayer

Grace, which empowers us to be hearers of the Word, is always given in and through the community; it is, indeed, God's love, but the incarnate God's, whose will it is to do nothing otherwise than in communion with his brethren. . . . The community is an essential factor in God's Word and in the hearer of it.

—Hans Urs von Balthasar

HISTORY OF COMMUNAL PRAYER

In the Gospel of Matthew, Jesus tells his disciples "where two or three are gathered in my name, there I am among them" (Matt. 18:20). Christian prayer begins and ends in community. As Keith Egan and Lawrence Cunningham say in their book *Christian Spirituality*: "We are most church when we gather as an assembly."

THE HOUSE CHURCH

Communal prayer has been with us almost as long as civilization itself. Since ancient times, people have joined together in worship of the gods (and later, in monotheistic faiths, the one God).

Christian communal worship grew out of the Jewish liturgical tradition. Jesus and his disciples would often attend the synagogue and participate in the Jewish service. Only when the Christian community began inviting and baptizing Gentiles into the faith without circumcision did they become a distinct group from within the Jewish faith.

Christian worship then moved to the private homes of the faithful, where believers would gather to "break bread" and celebrate their newfound faith. These smaller services imitated Jewish synagogue worship in that they involved prayers, readings, preaching, and the celebration of the Eucharist.

EUCHARIST

The term "to break bread" has been used in connection with the celebration of the Eucharist since the time of Jesus. Throughout the gospels, Jesus is often sharing a meal with his disciples, in which he begins by breaking bread. This was customary in Palestine at the time: the host would introduce the main course of a meal by breaking bread. Jesus incorporated this custom into the first Christian prayer services with his disciples. The Last Supper is especially meaningful in this context.

> While they were eating, he took a loaf of bread, and after blessing it he broke it, gave it to them, and said, "Take; this is my body." (Mark 14:22)

Breaking bread soon became the way of introducing the commemorative meal in the prayer services of the early Christian community. The term then came to mean the meal itself. The Acts of the Apostles in the New Testament describes the first Christian communities:

> They devoted themselves to the apostles' teaching and fellowship, to the breaking of bread and the prayers. (Acts 2:42)

The Book of Acts, then, is not describing Christians coming together for a common meal; it is referring to the celebration of the Eucharist—a special meal by which to remember and reenact the Lord's Supper. John Wright writes in *A Theology of Christian Prayer*:

> Breaking bread as an isolated gesture has no liturgical significance, but as introducing and designating the entire celebration of the Lord's Supper, it refers to the heart of the Christian liturgy.

LITURGY

The four primary elements of the first Christian worship service—prayers, readings, preaching, and the celebration of the Eucharist—still constitute the basic framework of the Christian liturgy today. John Wright describes the place of each component in early Christian worship:

> **Prayers** included formal prayers, like the Lord's Prayer, psalms from the Old Testament, and prayers offered "through Christ" to which the congregation responded "Amen" (2 Cor. 1:20). But there were also spontaneous prayers,

including prayers in tongues. And we should mention here the songs and spiritual canticles that were so often a part of Christian prayer together.

Readings were drawn first of all from the Old Testament, since Christians were profoundly aware of the fulfillment of those writings in their own history. . . . In addition letters written to a particular church by an apostle were not only read in that church, but exchanged with others as well. Accounts of the words and works of Jesus were probably first stylized in oral tradition and then written down to be read when Christians came together to celebrate the good news. Our four written gospels all bear marks of liturgical influences in their origin.

Preaching, teaching, prophecy, speaking in tongues and interpreting tongues, were all integral parts of the Christian worship. . . . The word of God lived in the intercommunication within the Christian Church.

Finally, there was the **celebration of the Eucharist**. Several expressions in Lucan writings suggest that in some places at least, this was a daily occurrence. . . . This eucharistic meal was not just sharing a meal together with Jesus, it was "proclaiming the Lord's death until he comes" (1 Cor. 11:26). Furthermore, it was a renewal of the covenant, of the new covenant in the blood of Jesus.

THEOLOGY OF COMMUNAL PRAYER

I begin and end our discussion on the theology of communal prayer with eucharistic and liturgical prayer because in these two elements are found all other aspects of prayer.

EUCHARISTIC PRAYER

"Eucharistic prayer is the deep center and firm matrix from which all other Catholic prayer arises," writes Lawrence Cunningham in *Catholic Prayer*. However, to appreciate his statement we must understand eucharistic prayer in the context of Catholic prayer. Cunningham helps us with this when he explains:

> Eucharistic prayer is Catholic prayer when we learn to celebrate the real presence of Christ in the Eucharist as our Lord and Savior while affirming our unity with the entire church, symbolized by our Communion at the liturgy and our will to unite ourselves with, in the words of the liturgy, "our absent brethren."

Cunningham goes on to say that "the essential heart of Catholic prayer is the Eucharist." Moreover, true Catholic prayer happens in the communal setting of the Eucharist.

Even when we pray privately, which I will address in the next chapter, we pray in the context of the Eucharist. In the remembrance and reliving of the Lord's Supper is shaped all other forms and methods of Christian and Catholic prayer.

> The Eucharist, at the very heart of the Catholic reality, is sacramental, incarnational, and the vehicle of making present the living Christ in time and space. It is from those characteristics as we encounter them in our faith experience of the living Christ that should (or better, must) shape and energize all of our other prayer. As we privately pray in adoration, thanksgiving, penitence, or petition we do so in our own words and according to our impulses. Nonetheless, overarching those private moments with God there is the deeply real presence of Christ, encountered in the Eucharist, that keeps us within the mind and intentions of Christ. It is from that center that all prayer should radiate. (*Catholic Prayer*)

In *Foundations of Christian Faith*, the late German theologian Karl Rahner said that "the sacrament of the Eucharist should not simply be counted among the seven sacraments." The Eucharist, in his eyes, is much more than a sacrament. In the following passages, he describes the unique place of the Eucharist in the Church.

KARL RAHNER
THE EUCHARIST

- The sacrament of the Eucharist should not simply be counted among the seven sacraments. However much it involves the individual and brings him time and time again into the community with Christ, it is nevertheless the sacrament of the church as such in a very radical sense. It is precisely the institution of the Lord's Supper which is of decisive importance for the founding of the church and for the self-understanding of Jesus as the mediator of salvation.

- In the celebration and reception of the Eucharist the church and the individual believer really give "thanks," which is what "Eucharist" means, and they do this in the fullest possible and "ecclesial" way which is only possible for the church of Jesus Christ.

- In the Eucharist the gratuitous and irrevocable salvific will of God for all men becomes present, tangible and visible *in* this world insofar as through the Eucharist the tangible and visible community of believers is fashioned into *that* sign which does not only point to some possible grace and salvific will of

God, but rather *is* the tangibility and the permanence of this grace and this salvation. It is obvious, therefore, that, insofar as the Eucharist is the sacrament of the most radical and most real presence of the Lord in this celebration in the form of a meal, the Eucharist is also the fullest actualization of the essence of the church. For the church neither is nor wants to be anything else but the presence of Christ in time and space. And insofar as everyone participates in the same meal of Christ, who is the giver and the gift at the same time, the Eucharist is also the sign, the manifestation and the most real actualization of the church insofar as the church is and makes manifest the ultimate unity of all men in the Spirit, a unity which has been founded by God in grace.

—*Foundations of Christian Faith*

LITURGICAL PRAYER

> We can pray individually with great integrity, but we can pray as Catholics only by participation in the liturgy and, further, that basic prayer needs to involve all other prayers. (*Catholic Prayer*)

The word *liturgy* comes from the Greek term *leitourgia*, meaning "work of the public." The liturgy is "the public and official prayers and rites of the Church" (*Encyclopedia of Catholicism*). It is the celebration of worship by the "People of God" (*Dogmatic Constitution on the Church,* Vatican Council II).

The liturgy is essentially a communal act. It is the activity of a whole community, united by faith in a triune God. As Lawrence Cunningham points out, it is in the communal nature of the liturgy that its catholicity or "universality" is found:

> The communal nature of this primordial act of worship [celebration of the Eucharist] needs to be underscored because it is there that the fullest sense of catholicity is present. The Catholic concept of faith is not a vertical model in which there is myself and God to the exclusion of the community, in the sense that we are called into the New Covenant whose pledge is Christ. In fact, as the unbroken testimony of the church's witness testifies,

> every small community (e.g., a parish) is a microcosm (the *ecclesiola*) of the whole bond of believers whom we call the Communion of Saints. There is, in short, no genuine Catholic life of prayer unless it is rooted in the gathered celebration of the mysteries of Jesus Christ in the liturgy. (*Catholic Prayer*)

As he points out later, the early Christian community "saw the intimate connection between the celebration of the liturgy and the extended lives of the community." Karl Rahner underscores this idea of communal interdependence or accountability in his "Prayer for the Church."

> I shall pray for the Church, my God, each day during the celebration of the Eucharist. My faith can only survive in the community of those who together form the holy Church of Jesus Christ. And therefore . . . it is essential to my own salvation that she be the very home and foundation of my faith.
>
> I know of course that she always is and always will be this for me through the power of Your tender mercy. Yet because she is also the Church of poor sinners she can only serve as a foundation and a dwelling place to an entirely different extent: she can make it easier or more difficult for me to believe in You and in Your victorious love for me. (*Prayers for a Lifetime*)

HANS URS VON BALTHASAR
LITURGY—CELEBRATION OF GOD'S PRAISE

- What liturgy on the part of human beings would be worthy of the object of its reverence, before which even in heaven every being casts itself upon its face, removes its wreaths and crowns, and places them in a gesture of worship before the throne of God: "You alone, O Lord, our God, are worthy of praise, honor and power" (Rev. 4:11)? This heavenly giving back of every good received by creatures to the one "who has made everything by his will" can compel an earthly community made up of sinners on its knees from the start to a *Domine, non sum dignus*.

- In a purely monotheistic religion the gesture of *proskynesis* (kneeling and bowing) is the most perfect expression of the giving over of the entire person, even in a great assembly. What Christian cannot be deeply struck at contemplating the silently worshipping crowd in a mosque! In the religion of the covenant, the hearing of the word of God, the Torah, stands in the middle: God speaks, the human beings receive in obedience, seeking in their hearts how they might rightly respond. . . .

  But then, in the trinitarian religion, an unheard-of transformation occurs: from the arbitrary lamb eaten in the family circle into "the Lamb slaughtered from the beginning of the world," "which takes away the sins of the world" and gives his flesh and blood as "true food and true drink."

- Inasmuch as we receive [the Son of man] into ourselves, we remember that in his passion he has received us into himself. . . . "As often as you eat this bread and drink this cup, you proclaim the death of the Lord, until he comes again" (1 Cor. 11:26). And yet we are not supposed to approach embarrassed and downcast, for the Lord . . . does not want us to feel strange . . . but to open our souls for the gift of the Father. For our gaze at the celebration is not narrowed to Jesus, but raised to the One from whom the highest of all goods ultimately comes, to the Father; nor are we ourselves the ones to bring about this opening and raising, but the Holy Spirit of the Father and the son, who is poured out into our hearts. The worshipping community, which celebrates God's generosity and liberality, is gathered for the triune God and nothing else.

—The von Balthasar Reader

COMMUNAL PRAYER TODAY

Since the Second Vatican Council, there have been many changes made to the liturgy. Worship has become more assembly-oriented (versus presider-oriented) with the language changing from Latin to the vernacular, and the assembly playing a more active role in the service.

LITURGICAL REFORM

The Church of today, as described in the conciliar documents (Vatican Council II), encourages active participation of the whole community in an effort to create a prayer service that imitates more closely the communal worship of the first Christian communities:

> The Church, therefore, earnestly desires that Christ's faithful, when present at this mystery of faith, should not be there as strangers or silent spectators. On the contrary, through a good understanding of the rites and prayers they should take part in the sacred action, conscious of what they are doing, with devotion and full collaboration. (*Constitution on the Sacred Liturgy*, no. 48)

VATICAN COUNCIL II
THE CONSTITUTION ON THE SACRED LITURGY

- In the earthly liturgy we take part in a foretaste of that heavenly liturgy which is celebrated in the Holy City of Jerusalem toward which we journey as pilgrims. . . . With all the warriors of the heavenly army we sing a hymn of glory to the Lord; venerating the memory of the saints, we hope for some part and fellowship with them; we eagerly await the Saviour, Our Lord Jesus Christ, until he our life shall appear and we too will appear with him in glory.

- The liturgy is the summit toward which the activity of the Church is directed; it is also the fount from which all her power flows. For the goal of apostolic endeavor is that all who are made sons of God by faith and baptism should come together to praise God in the midst of his Church, to take part in the Sacrifice and to eat the Lord's Supper.

- From the liturgy . . . and especially from the Eucharist, grace is poured forth upon us as from a fountain, and the sanctification of men in Christ and the glorification of God to which all other activities of the Church are directed . . . are achieved with maximum effectiveness.

INFORMAL PRAYER

It should be said that the celebration of the Eucharist is not the only form of communal worship that the Church provides; there are many other ways in which the faithful can gather together and pray.

Many people find it helpful to meet in "small faith communities," where persons read and discuss one or more Scripture passages, meditate, and pray. Similarly, there are prayer groups, Bible studies, and reading groups that help nurture the faith life of believers. The Liturgy of the Hours (or Divine Office), one of the oldest devotions of the Catholic faith, is a more formal prayer of the Church. By offering praise to God at different hours, a person sanctifies his or her entire day.

The Church encourages all forms of prayer, but only to the extent that they are derived and contribute back to the liturgy:

> Popular devotions of the Christian people, provided they conform to the laws and norms of the Church, are to be highly recommended. . . . But such devotions should be drawn up that they . . . accord with the sacred liturgy, are in some way derived from it, and lead the people to it, since in fact the liturgy by its very nature is far superior to any of them. (*Constitution on the Sacred Liturgy*, no. 13)

CHAPTER FOUR

PRIVATE PRAYER

Whenever you pray, go into your room and shut the door and pray to your Father who is in secret; and your Father who sees in secret will reward you.

—*Matthew 6:6*

HISTORY OF PRIVATE PRAYER

Although liturgical prayer is superior to private prayer in the sense that the liturgy is the public and official prayer of the Church, both are important in the spiritual lives of the faithful. The *New Catholic Encyclopedia* states:

> There exists the greatest harmony between private prayers and liturgical prayer, and both are necessary if Christ is to be formed in man. Consequently, private devotions may be considered as aids to the liturgical cult. Through them the Christian is prepared to offer the Sacrifice of the Mass with better dispositions, to receive the Sacraments with more fruit, and to participate in the sacred rites with greater fervor and recollection.

PRIVATE PRAYER IN THE GOSPELS

By his example, Jesus teaches us the importance of private prayer. At the beginning and throughout his public life, he often went away by himself to pray.

One of the first examples of Jesus praying occurs in the Gospel of Luke, after he had been baptized by John.

> Now when all the people were baptized, and when Jesus also had been baptized and was praying, the heaven was opened, and the Holy Spirit descended upon him in a bodily form like a dove. And a voice came from heaven, "You are my Son, the Beloved; with you I am well pleased." (Luke 3:21-22)

Another significant time of prayer is when Jesus withdrew to the wilderness for forty days and forty nights to fast and pray in preparation for his public ministry.

There are many times throughout his earthly ministry that Jesus sought time alone with his Father. Private prayer became increasingly more important for our Lord as word spread about his miracles and crowds surrounded him wherever he went. In the fifth chapter of Luke we read:

> Now more than ever the word about Jesus spread abroad; many crowds would gather to hear him and to be cured of their diseases. But he would withdraw to deserted places and pray. (Luke 5:15-16)

Occasionally, he would spend whole nights in prayer, as is described in Luke 6:12:

> Now during those days he went out to the mountain to pray; and he spent the night in prayer to God.

THEOLOGY OF PRIVATE PRAYER

When people speak of private prayer, they are usually referring to the kind of prayer that is done by oneself quietly or silently. Technically, it belongs under the classification of mental prayer, which includes meditation and contemplation, two prayer forms that are addressed in the next chapter.

MEDITATION

Since private prayer is most often a practice of meditation, it is important to briefly define meditation here; however, we will discuss it in more depth in the next chapter.

The *Encyclopedia of Catholicism* defines meditation as the "mental prayer of surrendered silence and listening." In her article "Prayer," Margaret Dorgan explains that meditative practices should move gradually from an intellectual mode to an affective mode:

> Thinking decreases and the heart is easily aroused to fervor. . . . Eventually affective prayer simplifies even more and is increasingly drawn to interior stillness. The multiplicity of acts by mind or heart are silenced into one single act of longing that is more like a state of

> being. This stage is aptly called the prayer of simplicity. Other names given to it are the prayer of faith, of repose, of simple regard, or of the simple presence of God. (*Encyclopedia of Catholicism*)

PRAYER OF QUIET

When a person meditates, he or she may use the language of Scripture—such as the psalms—or the words of a prayer, like the Lord's Prayer or the Hail Mary. Sometimes the pray-er may use literature from the saints or classic spiritual texts to facilitate the inward movement of private prayer.

Often, however, a person wishes to pray silently, without words—to merely sit still with God. In the following passage, Lawrence Cunningham and Keith Egan describe this kind of prayer, which is sometimes referred to as the "prayer of quiet":

> We have words like the "prayer of simplicity" or "contemplative prayer" or "mystical prayer" or the "prayer of quiet"—all terms which point to an experience that every believer may have experienced: a moment when words are simply not enough, and, by leaving aside words, one is simply in the presence of the Lord. Those experiences may come naturally or they may be

> consciously waited for, but they make up some of the deepest prayer experiences to which people of all ages and stripes have given witness. St. John Vianney, the patron saint of parish priests, once asked an old peasant whom he saw sitting in church each evening what he was doing. The farmer replied: "I look at the Good God [*Le Bonne Dieu*] and the Good God looks at me." That is about as good a description as one can articulate of this silent prayer, which so easily leads to contemplation. (*Christian Spirituality*)

The *New Catholic Encyclopedia* defines the prayer of quiet as:

> an intimate awareness of the presence of God that captivates the will and often fills the body and soul with ineffable sweetness and delight.

This article goes on to quote St. Teresa of Avila, who, in her autobiography, describes the prayer of quiet:

> This state is a recollecting of the faculties within the soul . . .; the will alone is occupied in such a way that, without knowing how, it becomes captive; the other two faculties [i.e., intellect and memory] help the will so that it may become more and more capable of enjoying so great a blessing. . . .

PRAYER AS WAITING

Not all private prayer is full of such affection and blessing; the prayer of quiet happens as a result of "fidelity to the practice of mental prayer and by cultivation of purity of life" (*New Catholic Encyclopedia*). Often in the process of sitting still with God, we just wait—and this waiting is sometimes painful, as it may seem to last into eternity. Karl Rahner beautifully articulates the waiting that is part of all prayer:

> This, then, is the ultimate meaning of my daily prayers, this awful waiting. It's not what I feel or think of in them, not the resolutions I make, not any superficial activity of my mind and will that You find pleasing in my prayer. All that is only the fulfillment of a command and, at the same time, the free gift of Your grace. All that is only clearing the ground, so the soul will be ready for that precious moment when You offer it the possibility of losing itself in the finding of You, of praying itself into You.
>
> Give me, O God of my prayer, the grace to continue waiting for You in prayer. ("God of My Prayer," *Prayers for a Lifetime*)

TERESA OF AVILA
PRAYER OF QUIET

In the following passage, St. Teresa of Avila compares the prayer of quiet to the story of Simeon, the prophet who, upon seeing the child Jesus in the temple, knew he had seen the Christ.

This prayer is something supernatural, something we cannot procure through our own efforts. In it the soul enters into peace or, better, the Lord puts it at peace by His presence, as He did to the just Simeon [Luke 2:21-38], so that all the faculties are calmed.

The soul understands in another way, very foreign to the way it understands through the exterior senses, that it is now close to its God and that not much more would be required for it to become one with Him in union.

This is not because it sees Him with the eyes either of the body or of the soul. The just Simeon didn't see any more than the glorious, little, poor child. For by the way the child was clothed and by the few people that were in the procession, Simeon could have easily judged the babe to be the son of poor people rather than the Son of our heavenly Father. But the child Himself made Simeon understand.

And this is how the soul understands here, although not with as much clarity. For the soul, likewise, fails to understand how it understands. But it sees it is in the kingdom, at least near the King who will give the kingdom to the soul. And seemingly the soul has so much reverence that it doesn't even dare ask for this. The state resembles an interior and exterior swoon; for the exterior man (or so that you will understand me better, I mean the body) doesn't want any activity. But like one who has almost reached the end of his journey he wants to rest so as to be better able to continue; in this rest his strength for the journey is doubled.

—*The Way of Perfection*

PRIVATE PRAYER TODAY

Because private prayer is informal in nature, there is no one way an individual goes about it. A person may have a certain time set aside in the morning or evening for quiet prayer. He or she may pray spontaneously, whenever the desire comes. And there are times—such as in personal crises—when we spend many hours of our day in private prayer.

A PRAYER PLACE

> Let there always be quiet, dark churches in which men can take refuge. Places where they can kneel in silence. Houses of God, filled with His silent presence. There, even when they do not know how to pray, at least they can be still and breathe easily. Let there be a place somewhere in which you can breathe naturally, quietly, and not have to take your breath in continuous short gasps. A place where your mind can be idle, and forget its concerns, descend into silence, and worship the Father in secret. (Thomas Merton in *New Seeds of Contemplation*)

As Thomas Merton describes so beautifully in the above passage, it is important for us to have a special place to go for prayer. Just as the earliest

JOYCE HUGGETT
A PRAYER PLACE

If you have already established a prayer corner or a prayer room, or if you have ever visited a building which is reserved for quiet prayer, you will understand why Jesus insisted that those who are serious about learning to pray should create a prayer place.

Places which are earmarked for prayer seem to be saturated with a sense of the presence of God. This powerful, prayerful atmosphere accumulates over the years and the more you visit such a place, the more you are drawn into the grand silence of God which seems to permeate every nook and cranny of the building or hover over the trees and glades and meadows or beach. Such places give rise to a heightened sense of expectancy, helping you to believe that you will encounter the God who seems to have taken up residence here in a very special way. In such places, you become acutely aware that God is there, greeting you, listening to you, blessing, restoring, nourishing and refreshing you.

—*Learning the Language of Prayer*

Christians set aside space in their homes for quiet reflection, some families today have prayer rooms or prayer corners—holy places reserved for prayer.

A prayer place doesn't necessarily have to be inside. Nature provides us with beautiful and inspiring settings for personal prayer. It is often easier to find a peaceful place outside—such as a clearing in the woods, or a sitting area by a creek—than to fight the distractions at home.

Since Jesus was homeless during most of his public life, he was always searching out places in nature to rest and pray. The Garden of Gethsemane was one of these special places, as is recorded in the Passion narratives. Our Lord also went off to the "wilderness" (Luke 4:1) and to the "mountain" (Luke 6:12) to pray.

POPULAR DEVOTIONS

For those who need a little more structure to their private prayer, there are private or popular devotions of the Church—such as the Rosary and the Stations of the Cross—that are more formulaic in nature. Many persons say prayers in devotion to the Blessed Mother and/or to the saints as part of their private worship. Personal novenas, pilgrimages, and the use of icons and sacred art also belong under the category of popular devotions.

CHAPTER FIVE

Meditation and Contemplation

Contemplation is the highest expression of man's intellectual and spiritual life. It is that life itself, fully awake, fully active, fully aware that it is alive. It is spiritual wonder.

—Thomas Merton

HISTORY OF MEDITATION AND CONTEMPLATION

In the last chapter we mentioned the "prayer of quiet" that happens as the inner stirrings of mind and heart are silenced into "one single act of longing" (*Encyclopedia of Catholicism*). This interior stillness is meditation that leads to contemplation; thus, last chapter's description of the prayer of quiet serves as an appropriate entry point into this chapter's discussion of meditation and contemplation.

MEDITATION AND CONTEMPLATION

As mentioned briefly in the introduction to this book, the terms *meditation* and *contemplation* are often used interchangeably. However, the two words point to two different experiences of prayer, as is suggested in the etymology of both words.

The word *meditation* comes from the Greek term *meletei*, meaning "care, study, exercise." In this sense, meditation is preparation for the gift of pure prayer, or contemplation.

The word *contemplation* is derived from the Latin *templum* or *tempus*, meaning "a division or section of time." This Latin term referred to the space in the sky or on the earth marked off for the Romans to read the omens. *Templum* later came to mean a sacred space to study and observe animals to discover divine meanings. Both Latin and Greek origins of the word point to the "regarding of beauty," or "study of the source," which, in effect, is God.

The basic distinction between meditation and contemplation, as stated in the introduction, is that meditation involves discursive reasoning and consideration, while contemplation takes the believer beyond what the rational faculties can access; contemplation is often described as a "simple gaze of love."

If we were to think of prayer as a journey to union with God, we would meet meditation first on our journey. As mentioned earlier, prayer often moves from an intellectual or reasoning mode to an affective mode, and then on to a mode of being—of utter stillness before God, or simple regard. Because meditation involves both reason and affection, it prepares us for the gift of contemplation, which is the state of being or stillness before God.

So, meditation and contemplation are distinct but intimately connected. Discussion of one without mention of the other is nearly impossible. It is best, as Lawrence Cunningham and Keith

Egan assert in *Christian Spirituality,* to keep them "in creative tension with each other as part of an ongoing journey to union with God in love."

Since the history and theology of meditation and contemplation cannot be neatly separated from each other, I treat the two methods of prayer together in this chapter, keeping in mind that meditation is a means to and preparation for contemplative prayer.

THE *KATAPHATIC* AND *APOPHATIC WAY*

Two important figures in the shaping of meditative and contemplative prayer are the Eastern Fathers Origen (d. 254) and Gregory of Nyssa (d. 395). They represent two different strains in understanding meditation and contemplation.

Origen, the theologian of light, approached the spiritual journey to union with God as three steps toward illumination. William H. Shannon offers an excellent explanation of Origen's theology in his article, "Contemplation, Contemplative Prayer" in *The New Dictionary of Catholic Spirituality*:

> First, there is a moral illumination, a movement away from sin and a conversion to the virtues (*praxis*). Then there is the stage of natural contemplation (*theoria*), in which the soul

IMPORTANT WORKS ON MEDITATION AND CONTEMPLATION

- Origen (d. 254) *On Prayer*
- Gregory of Nyssa (d. 395) *Life of Moses*
- John Cassian (d. 435) *Conferences*
- Pseudo-Dionysius (fifth or sixth century) *The Divine Names* and *The Mystical Theology*
- Benedict of Nursia (d. 550) *Rule*
- Bernard of Clairvaux (d. 1153) *On Loving God* and *Sermons on the Canticle of Canticles*
- Guigo II (d. 1188) *The Ladder of Monks*
- Anonymous monk (fourteenth century) *The Cloud of Unknowing*
- Ignatius of Loyola (d. 1556) *Spiritual Exercises*
- Teresa of Avila (d. 1582) *The Way of Perfection* and *The Interior Castle*
- John of the Cross (d. 1591) *The Ascent of Mount Carmel* and *The Dark Night of the Soul*
- Thomas Merton (d. 1968) *Seeds of Contemplation*

> comes to see the created world in God. Finally there is the contemplation of God himself (*theologia*), which is a return to the beginning and a recovery of the likeness of God.

Shannon points out that "this is progressively a movement toward greater and greater light" (*The New Dictionary of Catholic Spirituality*). This movement toward illumination or light, as represented by Origen, has come to be known as the *kataphatic way*, the way of affirmation. One comes to know God by way of human experiences and the created world.

Gregory of Nyssa presents a wholly different paradigm for understanding meditative and contemplative prayer. His way, recognized as the *apophatic way*, or way of negation, approaches God in utter darkness. "No ideas, thoughts, words, or symbols can reach God, as God is in his own reality" (*The New Dictionary of Catholic Spirituality*).

In his *Life of Moses*, Gregory of Nyssa reverses Origen's three stages, so that a person moves from light to darkness.

> There is, first, Moses' experience of light (*phos*) in the burning bush episode of Exodus 3. Then there are his two ascents, each time into a deeper darkness: first the ascent into the darkness of the cloud (*nephele*) in Exodus 19

> and then into the thick darkness (*gnophos*) in Exodus 33, in which God is experienced but as unknown. (William Shannon in *The New Dictionary of Catholic Spirituality*)

EARLY MONASTICISM

In the early monastic period (fifth to twelfth centuries), meditation and contemplation were organized into a system of prayer that involved four stages: *lectio*, *meditatio, oratio*, and *contemplatio*. Laurence Freeman, O.S.B. explains this "unified vision of prayer":

> This sense of prayer began with *lectio*, a reading aloud and memorizing of Scripture in a way that integrated body and mind at prayer, as in the Jewish practice. Meditation [*meditatio*] was a stage of resting on the words of the text that led beyond the imaginative and rationalizing levels of the mind through *oratio*, in which a personal appropriation of the meaning was made, to *contemplatio*, which was a nonconceptual, thought-free state of being in God rather than talking to God or thinking about God. ("Meditation" in *The New Dictionary of Catholic Spirituality*)

The primary place of *lectio* or *lectio divina*—which implies the whole process of *lectio, meditatio, oratio*, and *contemplatio*—in the prayer lives of fifth- and sixth-century monks is evident in the writings of John Cassian (d. 435) and in the *Rule* of Saint Benedict of Nursia (d. 550). Moreover, this monastic practice prepared the monk to offer his every day, his entire living, as a prayer before God. In his *Conferences*, John Cassian says to desert monks Isaac and Germanus:

> This, I say, is the objective of all perfection, to have the soul so removed from all dalliance with the body that it rises each day to the things of the spirit until all its living and all its wishing become one unending prayer.

Cassian, and later the anonymous author of *The Cloud of Unknowing*, advise the continuous recitation of a word or scriptural verse to "lead to peace beyond distraction and the self-centered consciousness of ego" (*The New Dictionary of Catholic Spirituality*).

MEDIEVAL SPIRITUALITY

Monastic life, like the secular world, was affected by a scholasticism that plagued Western thought in the late eleventh and twelfth centuries. However, due in part to the writings of Bernard of Clairvaux (d. 1153), the practice of *lectio divina* regained its important role in the prayer lives of monks.

The Carthusian Guigo II also contributed to the revival of *lectio divina* and to the development of meditative and contemplative prayer. In his *The Ladder of the Monks*, he outlines four steps to prayer: reading, meditation, prayer, and contemplation. He calls these the four rungs on the ladder to God.

THREE SPANISH MYSTICS

Finally, there are the Spanish mystics of the sixteenth century that would leave an enduring mark on the understanding of meditation and contemplation through their influential works. First there is Ignatius of Loyola (d. 1556), who, in his *Spiritual Exercises*, takes the reader or retreatant through a series of meditations and contemplations. There is Teresa of Avila (d. 1582), who teaches the prayer of recollection in her *The Way of Perfection*:

> This prayer is called "recollection," because the soul collects its faculties together and enters within itself to be with its God.

And there is Teresa's spiritual companion, John of the Cross (d. 1591), who concentrates on union with God in love in his *The Ascent of Mount Carmel* and *The Dark Night of the Soul*.

GUIGO II
THE LADDER OF MONKS

One day when I was busy working with my hands I began to think about our spiritual work, and all at once four stages in spiritual exercise came into my mind: reading, meditation, prayer and contemplation. These make a ladder for monks by which they are lifted up from earth to heaven.

It has few rungs, yet its length is immense and wonderful, for its lower end rests upon the earth, but its top pierces the clouds and touches heavenly secrets.

Just as its rungs or degrees have different names and numbers, they differ also in order and quality; and if anyone inquires carefully into their properties and functions, what each one does in relation to us, the differences between them and their order of importance, he will consider whatever trouble and care he may spend on this little and easy in comparison with the help and consolation which he gains.

Reading is the careful study of the Scriptures, concentrating all one's powers on it. ***Meditation*** is the busy application of the mind to seek with the help of one's own reason for knowledge of hidden truth. ***Prayer*** is the heart's devoted turning to God to drive away evil and obtain what is good. ***Contemplation*** is when the mind is in some sort lifted up to God and held above itself, so that it tastes the joys of everlasting sweetness.

You can see . . . how these degrees are joined to each other. One precedes another, not only in the order of time but of causality. Reading comes first, and is, as it were, the foundation; it provides the subject matter we must use for meditation. Meditation considers more carefully what is to be sought after; it digs, as it were, for treasure which it finds and reveals, but since it is not in meditation's power to seize upon the treasure, it directs us to prayer. Prayer lifts itself up to God with all its strength, and begs for the treasure it longs for, which is the sweetness of contemplation. Contemplation when it comes rewards the labors of the other three; it inebriates the thirsting soul with the dew of heavenly sweetness.

THEOLOGY OF MEDITATION AND CONTEMPLATION

As Laurence Freeman explains in his article "Meditation," Christian meditation is about turning "the consciousness of the person praying off self toward the divine Other" (*The New Dictionary of Catholic Spirituality*). Meditative and contemplative prayer involve a letting go of self to be united more fully in love with God.

SILENCE, STILLNESS, AND SIMPLICITY

Freeman goes on to describe three important components of the meditative and contemplative experience: silence, stillness, and simplicity:

> Silence is to be understood primarily as interior, the calming of the mind's noise and an awakening to the silent presence of God within. . . . Stillness in meditation leads to the knowledge of God (Ps. 46:10) through the integration of body and mind in the higher unity of the spirit. Simplicity is the most difficult because it involves the unfolding of consciousness from its habitual self-conscious and self-reflective state. . . . This radical quality of simplicity is the fruit by grace of sustained attention away from self and a

> discovery of one's true self inseparable from God, "in Christ." (*The New Dictionary of Catholic Spirituality*)

ACT OF FAITH AND LOVE

In meditation, which leads to the divine gift of contemplation, we commit an act of faith and an act of love.

> Meditation is an act of faith because it requires generous commitment and perseverance. It is an act of love, manifested in the growth of love in our life and in our relationships, because it turns us away from egoism toward the selflessness of the true self in Christ (Gal. 2:20). (*The New Dictionary of Catholic Spirituality*)

Moreover, meditation is "a way of interior sacrifice (Rom. 12:1-2) that allows the person to cooperate with the transforming and enlightening grace of Christ" (*The New Dictionary of Catholic Spirituality*). In this sense, meditation and contemplation invite the Christian to participate in Christ's redemptive and salvific gift to humanity.

> Meditation . . . is a spiritual path and discipline that leads to an encounter of our whole person with the redemptive holiness of Christ. (*The New Dictionary of Catholic Spirituality*)

THOMAS MERTON
NEW SEEDS OF CONTEMPLATION

Contemplation is the highest expression of man's intellectual and spiritual life. It is that life itself, fully awake, fully active, fully aware that it is alive. It is spiritual wonder. It is spontaneous awe at the sacredness of life, of being. It is gratitude for life, for awareness and for being. It is a vivid realization of the fact that life and being in us proceed from an invisible, transcendent and infinitely abundant Source. Contemplation is, above all, awareness of the reality of that source.

It *knows* the Source, obscurely, inexplicably, but with a certitude that goes both beyond reason and beyond simple faith. For contemplation is a kind of spiritual vision to which both reason and faith aspire, by their very nature, because without it they must always remain incomplete. Yet contemplation is not vision because it sees "without seeing" and knows "without knowing." It is a more profound depth of faith, a knowledge too deep to be grasped in images, in words or even in clear concepts. It can be suggested by words, by symbols, but in the very moment of trying to indicate what it knows the contemplative mind takes back what it has said, and denies what it has affirmed. For in contemplation we know by "unknowing." Or, better, we know beyond all knowing or "unknowing."

In other words, then, contemplation reaches out to the knowledge and even to the experience of the transcendent and inexpressible God. It knows God by seeming to touch Him. Or rather it knows Him as if it had been invisibly touched by Him. . . . Touched by Him Who has no hands, but Who is pure Reality and the source of all that is real! Hence contemplation is a sudden gift of awareness, an awakening to the Real within all that is real. A vivid awareness of infinite Being at the roots of our own limited being. An awareness of our contingent reality as received, as a present from God, as a free gift of love.

MEDITATION AND CONTEMPLATION TODAY

The prayer of meditation and contemplation, and especially the practice of *lectio divina*, were, until the second half of the twentieth century, mostly restricted to monastic life. However, the Second Vatican Council and the writings of Thomas Merton forged a religious renewal and a new appreciation for meditation and contemplation.

THOMAS MERTON

According to Lawrence Cunningham and Keith Egan, "no one has done more to liberate meditation and especially contemplation from . . . [religious] elitism than the Trappist monk Thomas Merton" (*Christian Spirituality*). Because Merton was read by so many people—not only priests, monks, and nuns—he introduced the meditative and contemplative experience to the laity. He formed a bridge between the spiritual practice that fed those in cloistered communities and the religious experience of the modern world.

Merton also helped heal the divide or seeming conflict between contemplation and action. In his work *Conjectures of a Guilty Bystander*, he describes an experience he had on a busy street corner of Louisville, Kentucky: suddenly he was overwhelmed with the love he had for the people on the street and felt a sincere connectedness to them.

UNIVERSAL CALL TO HOLINESS

Around the same time that Merton was bridging the gap between the modern religious experience and the ancient prayer of meditation and contemplation, the Second Vatican Council (1962-1965) issued its conciliar document *Lumen Gentium,* which calls everyone—laity and religious alike—to holiness:

> All in the Church, whether they belong to the hierarchy or are cared for by it, are called to holiness. . . . [This holiness of the Church] is expressed in many ways by the individuals who, each in his own state of life, tend to the perfection of love, thus helping others to grow in holiness. (*Dogmatic Constitution on the Church*, no. 39)

Thus, the spiritual exercises that were once assigned to members of religious communities are extended in this document to the entire "People of God" (*Dogmatic Constitution on the Church*, no. 9).

CENTERING PRAYER

Our discussion of meditation and contemplation would be incomplete without mention of Centering Prayer, a method of prayer that originated with John Cassian, Abba Isaac—a Desert Father of fourth-century Egypt—and Benedict of Nursia, and continued in the writings of St. John of the Cross and in the anonymous work *The Cloud of Unknowing*.

Following the example of Thomas Merton, spiritual leaders such as Cistercian monks Thomas Keating and M. Basil Pennington have introduced Centering Prayer to the modern world.

Thomas Keating explains how Centering Prayer fits into the contemplative experience. The following passage appears in his classic *Intimacy with God*:

> [Centering Prayer] bring us into the presence of God and thus fosters the contemplative attitudes of listening and receptivity. It is not contemplation in the strict sense, which in Catholic tradition has always been regarded as pure gift of the Spirit, but rather it is a preparation for contemplation by reducing the obstacles caused by the hyperactivity of our minds and of our lives.

M. BASIL PENNINGTON
CENTERING PRAYER

Traditionally [Centering Prayer] has had many names. It is the culmination of *lectio* and so did not need a particular name. It is *contemplatio*. It is prayer in the heart; the mind, the attention, comes down into the heart and abides quietly there. To achieve this, Abba Isaac counseled Cassian to be content with the poverty of a single simple word. The author of *The Cloud of Unknowing* pressed this further: Choose a simple word, a single-syllable word is best, like "God" or "love." Choose a word that is meaningful to you, the meaning being: I am all yours, Lord. This little word is fixed in the mind. It represents God and only God. It abides there, keeping the mind and heart in God. Anything else that comes along is simply let go. This little word is our sole response, God is our sole care during this time of love. It is simple as that.

The word has its power and meaning, for it is the fruit of *lectio*. *Contemplatio* always presupposes *lectio*. All prayer is a response. God speaks to us. We allow his word to come alive in us. It forms us and calls us into ever deeper union. It transforms us until we have the mind and heart of Christ.

To facilitate the teaching and practice of this very traditional prayer form we have set it forth in three simple points. . . .

Here then is the simple traditional way of entering into contemplative prayer that comes to us through the centuries and is now set forth in a simple, practical "packaging":

Sit quietly, eyes gently closed.

1. Be in faith and love to God who dwells within.

2. Take up a love word and let it be gently present, supporting your being to God in faith-filled love.

3. Whenever, during the time of your prayer, you become aware of anything, simply, gently return to the Lord, with the use of your word.

At the end of the twenty minutes, let the prayer word go and let the Lord's Prayer (or some other favorite prayer) quietly pray itself within.

—*Awake in the Spirit*

CHAPTER SIX

Lectio Divina

Whenever we say the word "lectio," we actually imply a whole process or way of spirituality—a journey into God, deep into the inner life of the Trinity.

—M. Basil Pennington

HISTORY OF LECTIO DIVINA

Although the practice of *lectio divina* was treated briefly in the last chapter, it deserves its own chapter because of the paramount role it plays in the development of Christian spirituality.

HOLY READING

Lectio divina is a Latin term, meaning "divine reading" or "holy reading." The *Encyclopedia of Catholicism* defines it as a "meditative reading of Sacred Scripture leading to prayer." It can also refer to the holy reading of other spiritual literature, such as writings of the Church Fathers. All *lectio divina*, however, requires "prayerful reflection on the text leading to communion with God in prayer" (*The New Dictionary of Catholic Spirituality*).

A MONASTIC PRACTICE

As mentioned in the last chapter, the practice of *lectio divina*—as one of the oldest and most important forms of meditative and contemplative prayer—is found most commonly in early monastic literature, such as the *Rule of St. Benedict.*

In his article "Lectio Divina," Kevin W. Irwin describes the purpose of *lectio divina* as explained in the *Rule of St. Benedict*:

> *Lectio* includes reading, private prayer, and *meditatio*, with "meditation" meaning the memorization, repetition, and prayerful rumination ("chewing over") of texts as a stimulus to personal prayer. The desired result of application to *lectio divina* is a thorough assimilation of sacred truth and a life lived according to this truth. (*The New Dictionary of Catholic Spirituality*)

In his *Rule*, St. Benedict assigns daily periods of sometimes two to three hours to *lectio*. Much of this instruction is found in Chapter 48 of the *Rule*:

> Idleness is the enemy of the soul. Therefore, the brothers should have specified periods for manual labor as well as for prayerful reading.
>
> We believe that the times for both may be arranged as follows . . .

According to the Benedictine code, *lectio* became an important way to prepare for Easter, as even more time is assigned to *lectio* during the season of Lent.

> During the days of Lent, [the brothers] should be free in the morning to read until the third

> hour, after which they will work at their assigned tasks until the end of the tenth hour. During this time of Lent each one is to receive a book from the library, and is to read the whole of it straight through. These books are to be distributed at the beginning of Lent.

FOUR MOMENTS OF PRAYER

The four moments of prayer attached to the practice of *lectio divina* (outlined by M. Basil Pennington on the next page) are found in the twelfth-century work *The Ladder of Monks*, mentioned in the last chapter. In his treatise, the Carthusian monk Guigo II describes a spiritual ladder of four rungs, representing four distinct but interdependent stages of *lectio divina.*

It is important to underscore the relationship between these four moments of prayer. As part of his conclusion, Guigo II explains their interconnection:

> Reading without meditation is sterile, meditation without reading is liable to error, prayer without meditation is lukewarm, meditation without prayer is unfruitful, prayer when it is fervent wins contemplation, but to obtain it without prayer would be rare, even miraculous. (*The Ladder of Monks*)

M. BASIL PENNINGTON
LECTIO DIVINA

• *Lectio*

This first element refers to the gathering of the Sacred Text and the plucking of the Word that we will use all day to remember God's message to us.

• *Meditatio*

The Word, coming to live in us through meditation, transforms our listening. Yes, we see Christ in the least, in everyone. And we know the joy of loving and serving him in each.

• *Oratio*

Almost naturally, this ongoing meditation calls forth again and again a response: thanksgiving, praise, petition, repentance, adoration. How present is God in all and acting through all.

• *Contemplatio*

There is something wonderful about a deep love, the love after the uncontrolled passion is spent. It is the love of just *being with*. This is contemplation.

THEOLOGY OF LECTIO DIVINA

In his book *Sacred Reading: The Ancient Art of Lectio Divina*, Michael Casey presents three themes in the theology of Scripture reading that will help us to better understand the practice of *lectio divina*. I discuss these themes in the following paragraphs.

LECTIO: A MEANS TO CONTEMPLATION

Casey first explains the role of *lectio* in leading us to prayer, and eventually to contemplation. He defines contemplation in the context of *lectio divina*:

> *Lectio divina* is an essential element in the flowering of contemplation. What is contemplation? It is a change in consciousness marked by two elements. On the one hand, there is a recession from ordinary sensate and intellectual awareness and all the concerns and programs that depend on it. At the same time, more subtly, it is being possessed by the reality and mystery of God. (*Sacred Reading*)

In reading Scripture, our minds and hearts are formed in and according to Christ; we are changed by grace as a result of our meditative reading.

Moreover, Casey asserts, "our actions can be vehicles of grace" when "our consciousness is shaped to agree with that of Christ" (*Sacred Reading*).

It is thus the role of *lectio divina* to shape our consciousness and transform our mind and heart so that we become in word and deed instruments of God's divine love and grace. Casey compares *lectio divina* to a school, in which Christ is both the master and the subject to be learned:

> [*Lectio divina*] is a school in which we learn Christ. In any master-disciple relationship, the content of what is learned is less important than the relationship itself; it is the prolonged mutual presence that communicates to the disciple the spirit and style of the elder. *Lectio divina* helps us to encounter Christ, it initiates us into the way of Christ. . . . In Christianity, the Word of God is a person, not a book. (*Sacred Reading*)

THE BIBLE AND THE CHURCH

Because we most often think of *lectio* as a personal exercise of meditation, it is difficult to recognize its communal or ecclesial character. However, *lectio divina* was originally the term used for liturgical readings as part of the communal setting.

The practice of *lectio* recalls the intrinsic and interdependent relationship between Scripture and the Church. Michael Casey describes this important relationship:

> Mutuality exists between the Church and sacred Scripture. Historically the Scriptures were created, edited, preserved, disseminated, and explained by the Church. Without the Church there would be no Bible: . . . it is the product of the Church's inspired industry. At the same time, without the Bible there would be no Church. Without the proclamation of the good news in some form, oral or written, the Church would have no common faith to bind its adherents together. (*Sacred Reading*)

Casey goes on to say that Scripture needs to be read in the context of the Church, both local and universal. Furthermore, "*lectio divina* is always an encounter with the Church as sacrament" (*Sacred Reading*) because the reading of Scripture leads us toward communion with fellow believers here and now and with the communion of saints. In this way, lectio is a "unitive force" (*Sacred Reading*).

LECTIO AND INCARNATION

Discussion of the ecclesial nature of *lectio divina* leads us to Casey's final theological theme, what he calls the "abbreviated word," which is the Incarnation—God's word made known to us in earthen vessels, and especially in the person of Jesus Christ. Casey explains this "abbreviated word":

> The Church Fathers used to speak of the "abbreviated word," *verbum abbreviatum*, a phrase coined on the basis of several texts in the Latin translation of Isaiah. The divine word trimmed itself to our capacities. It did not appear in overwhelming power and splendor but in accessible human form. This was always the manner of God's revelation. It reached its peak in the incarnation, when the second person of the Trinity became subject to space and time and all other human limitations. In so many ancient Christmas sermons, wonderment is expressed that the Word should have become a speechless babe. . . .
>
> The Scriptures are God's word reduced to a measure of which we are capable. (*Sacred Reading*)

Then, in order to understand *lectio divina* in its fullest capacity, we need to place it in its proper context—within the history of Christian salvation and redemption. We read the Scriptures keeping in mind the truest sense of the Word of God, which is the Incarnation.

MICHAEL CASEY
SEVEN PRINCIPLES OF LECTIO DIVINA

• *Principle 1*

Lectio divina is aimed not at confirming and reinforcing our individual approach to life, but at breaking into our subjective world and enriching it from the outside, delivering us from the prejudices and limitations of closed convictions and ideology and exposing our lives to the fullness of revelation and not simply to that part which presently appeals to us.

• *Principle 2*

Lectio divina is a long-term activity. It is not a source of immediate gratification as much as general provisioning for life. Fidelity and constancy are most valuable adjuncts to such reading.

• *Principle 3*

Lectio divina is connected with our personal sense of vocation. The aim of our reading is to hear the call of God clearly and concretely in our present situation.

• *Principle 4*

Lectio divina applies the Word of God to our own life-situation, allowing revelation and experience to overlap.

• *Principle 5*

There is a certain purposelessness or gratuity about lectio divina which is reflected in the leisure and peace which surround it. Lectio divina is done in such a way that it may be punctuated by prayer.

• *Principle 6*

Reading is not merely an "inner" exercise. As far as possible our whole body should participate in lectio divina.

• *Principle 7*

When something is encountered in our lectio divina which particularly speaks to us we should endeavor to retain it in our memory lest any of its savor escape us.

—*The Undivided Heart*

LECTIO DIVINA TODAY

There is a renewed interest in the practice of *lectio divina* in our day, as is evidenced by the number of books and articles circulating today on this and like topics.

CLASSIC TEXTS

Classic texts of Western spirituality—writings of the Desert Fathers, patristic texts, and ancient treatises on prayer—have resurfaced in religious circles, and have been introduced to lay believers, as important models to imitate for spiritual growth. Study of scripture passages is done today not only by theologians involved in scientific exegesis, but by those wanting to reflect on the texts as a devotional exercise.

SPIRITUAL WRITINGS TODAY

Today we can add to the name of Thomas Merton many spiritual writers who have introduced *lectio divina* to our world. Among them is Kathleen Norris, a lay Presbyterian woman who, in becoming a Benedictine oblate, has translated into simple language the religious experience of that community.

KATHLEEN NORRIS
LECTIO DIVINA

"Lectio divina" literally means "holy reading," and would not have been a scary word for me had my first encounters with it in monastic literature not made it sound like an esoteric practice that I could never hope to employ. The classic definitions of contemplative reading have their uses, but when I was just starting out as a Benedictine oblate, I found their talk of stages, and attaining evermore profound levels of meaning, thoroughly discouraging. It was as if I would have to evolve into a higher life form—or at least one with more patience and a longer attention span—in order to attempt lectio at all.

When I finally confessed my misgivings to the monk who was the abbey's oblate director, he informed me that as far as he was concerned, I was already doing lectio. He had found the practice evident in the poetry I was writing in response to the scriptures I encountered in the monastery's liturgy of the hours. His words lifted a burden from me, as I had become aware that the venerable practice of lectio is one of the core experiences of Benedictine life. He helped me to understand that it is a daily meditation on scripture in which one reads not for knowledge or information but to enhance one's life of faith. Thus, it is not a method but rather a type of free-form, serious play.

One might read a passage aloud, trying on different voices: Pilate's "What is truth?" as a sarcastic aside not requiring a response, or as a brief moment of wonder, inviting a response that does not come. One might attempt to memorize a verse or two of scripture and let it percolate through the consciousness while going about one's work, allowing the words to become a part of everyday life, illuminating one's relationships with others, and with the self.

—*Amazing Grace*

CHAPTER SEVEN

The Language of Prayer

Just as, when we attempt to learn a new language, we need to commit ourselves to the hard work of mastering the alphabet with its challenge to pronounce sounds correctly, so, when we attempt to learn the language of prayer, we need to be conversant with the equivalent of its ABC.

—*Joyce Huggett*

HISTORY OF THE LANGUAGE OF PRAYER

Since the beginning of civilization, people have searched for ways to express the presence of the divine in the world. The Hebrew Scriptures are filled with images and stories that articulate the unique covenant between God and humankind. Beautiful hymns abound in the Book of Psalms, the Book of Isaiah, and in the Song of Songs.

Words, symbols, and images are the media with which the authors of the Old and New Testaments describe the wonder of God.

LANGUAGE AND CULTURE

Language changes throughout time as the experiences of people change. Culture influences the words with which we speak to God. In *Catholic Prayer*, Lawrence Cunningham writes:

> When we wish to reach out in language to God it is both inevitable and natural that we should do so from the accumulated language of our own tradition. . . . We have at our disposal an entire vocabulary of prayer with which to start. It is only in the actual articulation of prayer that we begin to sift and choose that language

> which most appropriately connects to our own experience of faith.

CLASSIC PRAYERS

There are a number of prayers, however, that don't change: prayers which are as attached to a religious tradition as the creed itself. Cunningham notes, "The history of any religious tradition is very much a history of the conservation of hallowed prayers." We call these prayers "classics" because they offer enduring wisdom, insight for all ages. Lawrence Cunningham discusses the importance of the classic prayers within the Catholic tradition:

> The classic prayers of the Catholic tradition—the Lord's Prayer, the Ave Maria, etc.—have not exhausted their usefulness precisely because they remain in the tradition, give witness to its historicity, and are invoked in the very act of affirming that tradition. Such prayers, as it were, "frame" our lives as believers and as members of a faith community. We recite such prayers both because their authenticity is guaranteed by the tradition and because they "fit" the life we have assumed. (*Catholic Prayer*)

Classic prayers are able to speak to all generations not because they refrain from using language particular to a certain people and avoid touching on timely issues, but because their wisdom transcends the specific issues and language of that time. Moreover, the simplicity of the words used in classic prayers allows for a universal meaning. And in this way, they don't need to change, as Lawrence Cunningham explains:

> Prayers remain the same because their words in all their simplicity transcend the moment. Will the believer of the future not be able to say, like Isaiah, "Here am I. Send me"? Will the conditions of life change so much that the future believer will find the words of the psalmist irrelevant? Will we not need to cry out, "Though I am sometimes afraid, yet I put my trust in thee"? Will we not be able to cry out, as did Jesus using the words of the psalmist, "Into thy hands I commend my spirit"?
>
> Phrases and prayers like this transcend words or formula precisely because they bear behind them accumulated meanings that simply cannot be detached from the words themselves. (*Catholic Prayer*)

On the following pages are a handful of the classic prayers within our Catholic tradition.

CLASSIC PRAYERS

The Our Father

Our Father, who art in heaven,
hallowed be thy name;
thy kingdom come;
thy will be done on earth as it is in heaven.
Give us this day our daily bread;
and forgive us our trespasses,
as we forgive those who trespass against us;
and lead us not into temptation,
but deliver us from evil. Amen.

The Hail Mary

Hail Mary, full of grace,
the Lord is with thee.
Blessed art thou among women,
and blessed is the fruit of thy womb, Jesus.
Holy Mary, Mother of God,
pray for us sinners, now,
and at the hour of our death. Amen.

The Jesus Prayer

Lord Jesus Christ,
Son of the Living God,
Have mercy on me, a sinner.

The Apostles' Creed

I believe in God, the Father almighty,
creator of heaven and earth.
I believe in Jesus Christ, his only Son, our Lord.
He was conceived by the power of the Holy Spirit
and born of the Virgin Mary.
He suffered under Pontius Pilate,
was crucified, died, and was buried.
He descended into hell.
On the third day he rose again.
He ascended into heaven
and is seated at the right hand of the Father.
He will come again
to judge the living and the dead.
I believe in the Holy Spirit,
the holy catholic Church,
the communion of saints,
the forgiveness of sins,
the resurrection of the body,
and the life everlasting. Amen.

Grace Before Meals

Bless us, O Lord, and these your gifts
which we are about to receive from your bounty.
Through Christ our Lord. Amen.

The Doxology

Glory to the Father,
and to the Son,
and to the Holy Spirit;
as it was in the beginning,
is now,
and will be for ever. Amen.

The Regina Caeli

O Queen of heaven, rejoice! Alleluia.
For he whom you did merit to bear, Alleluia.
Has risen as he said. Alleluia.
Pray for us to God. Alleluia.

Rejoice and be glad, O virgin Mary, Alleluia.
For the Lord has risen indeed. Alleluia.

Let us pray:
O God, who gave joy to the world
through the resurrection of your Son
our Lord Jesus Christ,
grant that we may obtain,
through his virgin mother, Mary,
the joys of everlasting life.
Through the same Christ our Lord. Amen.

THEOLOGY OF THE LANGUAGE OF PRAYER

All language falls short of describing the experience of God—especially union with God in love—as we learned in Chapter Five, on the topics of meditation and contemplation. Prayer, after all, moves from words to silence, from thinking to being, from meditation to contemplation.

POETRY AS THEOLOGY

Poetry and symbolic language come as close as is possible for words in communicating the presence of God in our world. A poet, in finding language and symbols that connect with a people's experiences, illuminates the mystery of divine grace.

Poetry is a *locus theologicus*, a theological moment or place from which one can understand the divine in human life. Poetry helps one do theology because it fosters a better understanding of the experience of God.

PRIMORDIAL WORDS

Poetry is an appropriate language for God's self-communication because it employs what Karl

Rahner calls "primordial words" (*Urwortes*). Primordial words involve a transition, a transcendence of the spirit. Rahner says in his third volume of *Theological Investigations* that these words represent reality: "The object known is transferred into man's sphere of existence."

Furthermore, a primordial word completes or fulfills that which it describes. It puts objects into the light of knowledge and love. This word is spoken in the depths of the human person. It proclaims the infinity of God. The primordial word is, in fact, a significant sacramental expression.

Lawrence Cunningham offers a good commentary on an important essay of Rahner's, entitled "Priest and Poet," in which Rahner explains the use of primordial words in both ministries:

> Rahner appeals to . . . primordial words . . . whose use provides a door that opens into the unfathomable depths of true reality. The poet, like the priest, utters those words not in a scattered and uninformed manner but in what Rahner calls a "powerful concentration." In that calling forth of the primordial words, language brings forth the fundamental beauty of reality that stands in front of the unutterable mystery which is God. It is easy to see what Rahner means when we think of the deep power of

> words in the sacramental life of the church. Words forgive, heal, communicate, transubstantiate, and bind. (*Catholic Prayer*)

SYMBOLS AND PLAY

Both the poet and the priest use symbols as primordial words. According to Paul Tillich, "symbolic language alone is able to express the ultimate," (as quoted by John McKenna in the article "Symbol and Reality," *Worship* 65).

As primordial words, symbols make present what they symbolize. According to Rahner, a symbol is one reality that renders another present. An effective symbol produces insights into divine mystery so that both the symbol and reality become present and effective to the knower. However, in order to interpret symbols and use them to their fullest capacity, a person must develop a playful mind.

Play is the act of creation in concert with the imagination and reason; play engages a person in intellectual work while freeing the spirit for creativity. In play, a person uses reason within a relaxed and inspired context to find new interpretations or understandings.

It is important, then, that we use symbols and learn to be playful in our prayer.

THE LANGUAGE OF PRAYER TODAY

Although there are classic prayers and enduring symbols that will forever ground our faith in the Church of yesterday, there is always room for new language: words that translate the mystery of God to the modern experience.

LATIN TO VERNACULAR

Before the Second Vatican Council, when the Catholic Mass was said in Latin, persons who had studied the classical languages enjoyed a clear advantage over those with less education. The move to vernacular language indicated the Church's desire to invite all the faithful to participate in the liturgy, not just the learned.

INCLUSIVE LANGUAGE

Another significant change in religious language today is the shift toward inclusive language. With the feminist movement came the voices of men and women requesting that our language be revised to speak more directly to all the faithful, not just men. Several theologians have begun to use feminine terms to refer to God, encouraging fellow believers to think about God differently than our ancestors.

A NEW LOOK AT THE OLD

Sometimes it is helpful to revisit old words and images as we move throughout various stages in our life. Often we find new meaning and value in past treasures.

In her book *Amazing Grace*, Kathleen Norris chronicles her return to a vocabulary of faith that, at one point in her life, seemed dead:

> The vocabulary of a religious faith once seemed dead to me. In my college years I stumbled into poetry and found that its vocabulary served me very well; in fact, it became for many years a suitable substitute for religion. When I was in my twenties, any talk of religion generated a vague unease in me. . . . All that has changed. . . . In many ways, it is my accommodation of and reconciliation with the vocabulary of Christian faith that has been the measure of my conversion, the way in which I have entered and now claim the faith as my own.

CHAPTER EIGHT

The Body and Prayer

The greatest utility of bodies is in their use as signs. For from them are made many signs necessary for our salvation.

—Guigo II

HISTORY OF THE BODY AND PRAYER

The body is as important as speech in the language of prayer. B. I. Mullahy writes in his article "Liturgical Gestures":

> Bodily gestures are the principal means by which man expresses even the highest forms of his spiritual, intellectual, and artistic experiences, and the principal ways in which he communicates with the suprahuman, as well as the human and infrahuman world around him. . . . Gestures, no less than words, are a part of human language, the one appealing to the sight, the other to hearing—the two senses closest to the intellect and therefore closest to the spiritual life. (*New Catholic Encyclopedia*)

Words and gestures depend on each other for the "full expression of man's inner self" (*New Catholic Encyclopedia*). Gestures add intensity to words, while words give meaning to gestures.

CHRISTIAN PRAYER AND THE BODY

The body has been used by all religious traditions since the beginning of time as a medium of communication between the human and divine. In Christian prayer, the use of the body is especially meaningful since we believe that humans were made in the image and likeness of God, and because God became human in the Incarnation.

> Christian prayer demands a profound engagement of the human body, not only because of the composite and social nature of man, but also because the Word became flesh and gave man a share in the social life of the Trinity, expressed in the communal life of the Mystical Body. Thus the Christian, after the Incarnation, has a special reason for giving his sacramentalized body, destined for resurrection, a share in his prayer. (*New Catholic Encyclopedia*)

JESUS AS EXAMPLE

We learn the importance of bodily gestures from Jesus himself who raised his eyes to heaven (John 11:41) and fell to his knees (Luke 22:41) in praying to his Father.

B. I. Mullahy asserts that Jesus used bodily gestures throughout his ministry as a way of teaching. His life ends in a perfect gesture of sacrifice on the cross.

> The use of bodily gesture in the prayer life of the Church is simply an imitation of Christ Himself who in prayer lifted his eyes to heaven, prostrated Himself . . . ; who used gestures as a

> means to perform His miracles when a simple word would have sufficed; who taught by means of such gestures as the washing of the feet of His Disciples; and who finally offered His entire body in the perfect act of worship on the cross. (*New Catholic Encyclopedia*)

KINDS OF LITURGICAL GESTURES

There are a number of bodily gestures that have been adopted into the liturgical celebration of the Church. Mullahy classifies them into three groups:

> There are three ways in which the human body, through the use of gestures, enters into the liturgical action of the Church: by giving expression to the sentiments and dispositions of the soul, as in extending the hands, bowing, or striking the breast; by performing an action upon an external object, as in anointings and blessings; and by being acted upon in such a way that it becomes sanctified, as in baptismal immersion or the laying on of the hands. (*New Catholic Encyclopedia*)

Many of these gestures are found in ancient manuscripts, and have their origin in pagan practices. Others go back to the Old and New Testaments. On the following pages is a history of common liturgical gestures.

B. I. MULLAHY
HISTORY OF LITURGICAL GESTURES

• *Standing*

In antiquity . . . and for many centuries in the Church, standing was considered to be the most normal posture, and it is still so considered by the liturgy, except for times and ceremonies that call for a special expression of penance and humble adoration. . . .

For the early Christians, as for the pagans and the Jews, standing was a natural expression of respect and reverence. But for the Christians, as is evident in the writings of the Fathers, it had the added significance of the new dignity, the liberty of the children of God, the freedom from slavery and sin through Baptism and participation in the Resurrection, which makes it possible to stand confidently before God with eyes and arms uplifted to Him.

• *Sitting*

Sitting is a normal attitude for both speaker and listener. The Child Jesus was found seated in the midst of the doctors of the temple (Luke 2:46). Mary sat at the feet of Jesus listening to His words (Luke 10:39). There are indications in Scripture that, for both the Jews and the early

Christians, a sitting position was customary for listening to readings and the sermon, while standing was the usual practice for prayer. . . . Sitting has become a more common attitude of prayer in modern times, especially since pews were introduced into churches after the 16th century, as a result of the influence of the Reformation.

• *Kneeling*

Though it is especially in the last few centuries that kneeling has become the most popular position of the body in prayer, the almost instinctive practice of kneeling at prayer goes back to the Old Testament and is found in many pagan religions. This has been especially true in private prayer, and more particularly in times of especially intense prayer. . . . In the course of time, kneeling became more and more a sign of profound adoration, and this is now its predominant meaning. . . . Kneeling . . . has in modern times become the most characteristic attitude of prayer.

• *Genuflection*

The gesture of bending the knee is of ancient origin dating back to pre-Christian times. Its primary significance among the pagans, especially those of the Roman Empire, was that of adoration and worship, and it was used as a salutation to the gods and to the "divine" rulers, particularly the emperor. Because of this pagan religious significance, it was not used by the early Christians. When, however, it eventually lost this religious significance and began to be used simply as a sign of respect and courtesy for those in high authority, it was first used by Christians as a sign of reverence for popes and bishops, later for the altar, the crucifix, and relics and images of Christ and the saints.

• *Bows*

Bowing is a gesture that is, in a sense, something between standing erect and genuflecting, and it has, generally speaking, the same significance as the latter: humble supplication and above all adoration when directed toward God, reverence and veneration when directed toward men or objects. An instinctive expression of one's inner feelings and a common gesture in ancient pagan rites, it was introduced early into Christian prayer and became one of the most commonly used gestures in the liturgy, often on occasions for which genuflection has now been substituted in the Latin Church.

—*New Catholic Encyclopedia*

THEOLOGY OF THE BODY AND PRAYER

The theology of the human body with regard to prayer and the significance of liturgical gestures are found, as mentioned earlier, in the miracle of the Incarnation: God's becoming human in the person of Jesus Christ.

PRAYING WITH THE WHOLE SELF

The mystery of the Incarnation teaches us about the gift of our humanity—the integration of body, mind, heart, and soul in one person. In prayer, grace is bestowed on the whole person; prayer points all faculties—body, mind, spirit—towards their potential for good. Thus, it is important for us to pray with our whole being, our entire self; prayer is an exercise of the whole person.

Romano Guardini touches on the theological significance of gesture in *The Art of Praying*:

> Gesture reaches from the hand back to the heart. Outward bearing is rooted in inner attitude. It expresses what lives within, what the heart feels and the mind intends. Conversely it can itself affect the inner life, giving it stability and form.

ANTHONY DE MELLO
PRAYING BODY AND SOUL

- Prayer techniques are a means, not an end. If we attribute too much importance to the techniques, prayer becomes a sheer exercise for becoming physically or psychologically relaxed and nothing more.

- The body is part of our being and we must use it to become interiorly recollected. It is we who are praying, "soul and body" like Jesus, who while praying in the garden face down (Luke says: he "knelt down"), offers this prayer: "My Father, if it is possible, let this cup pass from me" (Matt. 26:39).

- The Bible and the liturgy situate the body at prayer. The masters of prayer say that "prayer methods" are like a drawbridge for entering a castle. It is true that no human technique, Zen, or yoga by itself attains the experience of God, union with God, contemplation. This goal of Christian prayer is sheer gift of God. It is as means that bodily and ascetical techniques acquire meaning. St. Teresa used to say, "We aren't angels, for we have a body."

- Another great master of prayer, St. Ignatius Loyola, recommends various body postures in the *Spiritual Exercises*: standing up, prostrate, kneeling, seated, lying down, and so forth, and one of his prayer methods is called "application of the senses": sight, hearing, taste, smell, touch.

EXERCISE

- St. Paul asks, "Do you not know that you are God's temple and that God's spirit dwells in you?" (1 Cor. 3:16). And the Psalmist presents the body as "the faithful collaborator and expression of our feelings:" (Ps. 69:3).

- Become aware that body and spirit make up a praying unit that can say with St. Augustine, "You have created me, Lord, for yourself, and my heart is restless until it rests in you."

- Rejoice in this reality, and while standing, lift up your hands expressing with our entire "Self" body-spirit, your thirst for the living God.

- Express spontaneously, through bodily gestures, our deepest feelings: wonder, satisfaction, joy, reverence, praise, adoration, thanksgiving.

- Find the way to express in gestures, with your hands, with looking, all these and other feelings that are welling up at this moment: sorrow, trust in God, surrender.

THE BODY AND PRAYER TODAY

There is a new appreciation in our day of the interrelationship of the body, mind, and spirit. The fields of medicine, psychology, and spirituality are learning from each other in the movement toward "wholistic" healing. Modern technology and science are able to show us just how much the spirit depends on the health of the mind and body, and vice versa.

LITURGICAL DANCE

This awareness has translated into creative ways of using the body to worship and pray. The growing popularity of various kinds of dance in the twentieth century has made liturgical dance acceptable in church settings today. Theatrical dance has returned to the church, as well, with the liturgical or sacred dance movement of this century.

PRAY ALWAYS

We can use our body in private prayer, as well. Since most of us keep a busy schedule, we need to learn how to pray during our "off" moments.

Thomas Merton offers a couple of ways in his *New Seeds of Contemplation*:

> Learn how to pray in the streets or in the country. Know how to meditate not only when you have a book in your hand but when you are waiting for a bus or riding a train.

Along this line, Keith Egan and Lawrence Cunningham write in *Christian Spirituality*:

> [Prayer] is an exercise of the whole person which is not incompatible with other activities such as walking or running or other forms of exercise. . . . Anything that integrates prayer or meditative reflection with other activities helps to integrate our ordinary pastimes with the life of prayer.

Many persons today devote a half-hour or an hour daily to prayer-walking, as is described by Linus Mundy in *Prayer-Walking: A Simple Path to Body-and-Soul Fitness*. This provides a consistent, peaceful moment in which the whole self is involved in prayer.

Works Cited

The following is a list of the books from which I have quoted in the preceding chapters.

Ayo, Nicholas, C.S.C. *The Lord's Prayer: A Survey Theological and Literary*. Notre Dame, Indiana: University of Notre Dame Press, 1992.

Boff, Leonardo. *The Lord's Prayer: The Prayer of Integral Liberation*. Maryknoll, New York: Orbis Books, 1983.

Brown, Raymond. "The Pater Noster as an Eschatological Prayer," *Theological Studies* 22 (1961): 208.

Casey, Michael. *Sacred Reading: The Ancient Art of Lectio Divina*. Liguori, Missouri: Liguori Publications, 1996.

Casey, Michael. "Seven Principles of Lectio Divina," *The Undivided Heart: The Western Monastic Approach to Contemplation*. Petersham, Massachusetts: St. Bede's Publications, 1994.

Cassian, John. *Conferences*. Mahwah, New Jersey: Paulist Press, 1985.

Catechism of the Catholic Church. Washington, D.C.: United States Catholic Conference, Inc.—Liberia Editrice Vaticana, 1994.

Cunningham, Lawrence S. *Catholic Prayer*. New York: The Crossroad Publishing Company, 1989.

Cunningham, Lawrence S. and Egan, Keith J. *Christian Spirituality: Themes from the Tradition*. Mahwah, New Jersey: Paulist Press, 1996.

De Mello, Anthony. *Praying Body and Soul*. New York: The Crossroad Publishing Company, 1997.

Downey, Michael, ed. *The New Dictionary of Catholic Spirituality*. Collegeville, Minnesota: The Liturgical Press, 1993.

Flannery, Austin, O.P., ed. *Vatican Council II, Volume 1, Revised Edition: The Conciliar and Post Conciliar Documents*. Northport, New York: Costello Publishing Company, 1998.

Guardini, Romano. *The Art of Praying: The Principles and Methods of Christian Prayer*. Manchester, New Hampshire: Sophia Institute Press, 1985.

Guardini, Romano. *The Lord's Prayer*. Manchester, New Hampshire: Sophia Institute Press, 1986.

Guigo II: The Ladder of Monks. Kalamazoo, Michigan: Cistercian Publications, 1981.

Huggett, Joyce. *Learning the Language of Prayer*. New York: The Crossroad Publishing Company, 1997.

Keating, Thomas. *Intimacy with God*. New York: The Crossroad Publishing Company, 1996.

McBrien, Richard P., ed. *The HarperCollins Encyclopedia of Catholicism*. San Francisco: HarperCollins, 1995.

McKenna, John. "Symbol and Reality: Some Anthropological Considerations," *Worship* 65 (January 1991), 2-27.

Merton, Thomas. *New Seeds of Contemplation*. New York: New Directions Books, 1961.

New Catholic Encyclopedia, Vol. 1 - Vol. 15. Washington, D.C.: Catholic University of America Press, 1967-79.

Norris, Kathleen. *Amazing Grace: A Vocabulary of Faith*. New York: Riverhead Books, 1998.

Pennington, Basil M. *Awake in the Spirit: A Personal Handbook on Prayer*. New York: The Crossroad Publishing Company, 1996.

Pennington, Basil M. *Lectio Divina: Renewing the Ancient Practice of Praying the Scriptures*. New York: The Crossroad Publishing Company, 1998.

Rahner, Karl. *Foundations of Christian Faith: An Introduction to the Idea of Christianity*. New York: The Crossroad Publishing Company, 1992.

Rahner, Karl. *Prayers for a Lifetime*. New York: The Crossroad Publishing Company, 1995.

The Rule of St. Benedict in English. Collegeville, Minnesota: The Liturgical Press, 1981.

Teresa of Avila, *The Way of Perfection*. Washington, D.C.: Institute of Carmelite Studies Publications, 1980.

Von Balthasar, Hans Urs. *Prayer*. New York: Sheed & Ward, 1961.

Von Balthasar, Hans Urs. *The von Balthasar Reader*. New York: The Crossroad Publishing Company, 1997.

Wright, John H., S.J., *A Theology of Christian Prayer*. New York: Pueblo Publishing Company, 1987.

Acknowledgments

We wish to acknowledge the following publishers for permission to reprint previously published material.

From *Amazing Grace* by Kathleen Norris. Copyright © 1998 by Kathleen Norris. Used by permission of Putnam Berkley, a division of Penguin Putnam Inc. Other rights, reprinted by permission of Janklow & Nesbit.

From *The Art of Praying* by Romano Guardini. Copyright © 1957, 1985 by Pantheon Books, A Division of Random House, Inc. Reprinted by permission of Sophia Institute Press.

From *A Theology of Christian Prayer* by John H. Wright. Copyright © 1979, 1987 by Pueblo Publishing Company, Inc. Reprinted by permission of John H. Wright.

From *Awake in the Spirit* by M. Basil Pennington. Copyright © 1992 by Cistercian Abbey of Spencer, Inc. Reprinted by permission of The Crossroad Publishing Company.

Excerpts from the English translation of the *Catechism of the Catholic Church*. Copyright © 1994, Libreria Editrice Vaticana—United States Catholic Conference, Inc. Used with permission.

From *Catholic Prayer* by Lawrence S. Cunningham. Copyright © 1989 by Lawrence S. Cunningham. Reprinted by permission of The Crossroad Publishing Company.

From *Christian Spirituality* by Lawrence S. Cunningham and Keith J. Egan. Copyright © 1996 by Lawrence S. Cunningham and Keith J. Egan. Used by permission of Paulist Press, Inc.

From *The Collected Works of St. Teresa of Avila* translated by Kieran Kavanaugh, O.C.D. and Otilio Rodriguez, O.C.D. Copyright © 1980 by Washington Province of Discalced Carmelites, Inc. Reprinted by permission of ICS Publications.

From *Foundations of Christian Faith* by Karl Rahner. English translation copyright © 1978 by The Crossroad Publishing Company. Reprinted by permission of The Crossroad Publishing Company.

From *Guigo II: The Ladder of Monks* translated by Edmund Colledge, O.S.A. and James Walsh, S.J. Copyright © 1978 by Edmund Colledge and James Walsh. Reprinted by permission of Cistercian Publications, Inc.

Excerpts as submitted from *The HarperCollins Encyclopedia of Catholicism* by Richard P. McBrien. Copyright © 1995 by HarperCollins Publishers, Inc. Reprinted by permission of HarperCollins Publishers, Inc.

From *Learning the Language of Prayer* by Joyce Huggett. Copyright © 1994 by Joyce Huggett. Reprinted by permission of The Crossroad Publishing Company. UK/Commonwealth rights, reprinted by permission of The Bible Reading Fellowship, Oxford, England.

From *Lectio Divina* by M. Basil Pennington. Copyright © 1998 by Cistercian Abbey of Spencer, Inc. Reprinted by permission of The Crossroad Publishing Company.

From *The Lord's Prayer* by Nicholas Ayo. Copyright © 1992 by University of Notre Dame Press, Notre Dame, IN, 46556. Reprinted by permission of University of Notre Dame Press.

From *The Lord's Prayer* by Romano Guardini. English translation copyright © 1958, 1986 by Random House, Inc. Reprinted by permission of Pantheon Books, a Division of Random House, Inc. and Sophia Institute Press.

From *New Catholic Encyclopedia* Vol. 1 -Vol. 15. Copyright © 1967-1979 by The Catholic University of America Press. Reprinted by permission of The Catholic University of America Press.

From *The New Dictionary of Catholic Spirituality* edited by Michael Downey. Copyright © 1993 by The Order of St. Benedict, Inc., Collegeville, Minnesota. Reprinted by permission of The Liturgical Press.

From *New Seeds of Contemplation* by Thomas Merton. Copyright © 1961 by The Abbey of Gethsemani, Inc. Reprinted by permission of New Directions Publishing Corp. UK/Commonwealth rights, reprinted by permission of Gerald Pollinger, Ltd.

From *Praying Body and Soul* by Anthony De Mello. English translation copyright © 1997 by The Crossroad Publishing Company. Reprinted by permission of The Crossroad Publishing Company.

From *Sacred Reading* by Michael Casey. Copyright © 1995 by Michael Casey. Reprinted by permission of Liguori Publications.

From *The Undivided Heart* by Michael Casey. Copyright © 1994 by Michael Casey. Reprinted by permission of St. Bede's Publications.

Excerpts from *Vatican Council II, Volume 1, Revised Edition: The Conciliar & Post Conciliar Documents* edited by Austin Flannery, O.P., copyright © 1998, Costello Publishing Company, Inc., Northport, NY are used by permission of the publisher, all rights reserved. No part of these excerpts may be reproduced, stored in a retrieval system, or transmitted in any form or by any means—electronic, mechanical, photocopying, recording or otherwise, without express permission of Costello Publishing Company.

From *The von Balthasar Reader* by Hans Urs von Balthasar. English translation copyright © 1982 by The Crossroad Publishing Company. Reprinted by permission of The Crossroad Publishing Company.